THE INTERNATIONAL MARINE
SAILBOAT LIBRARY

# INSPECTING THE AGING SAILBOAT

## DON CASEY

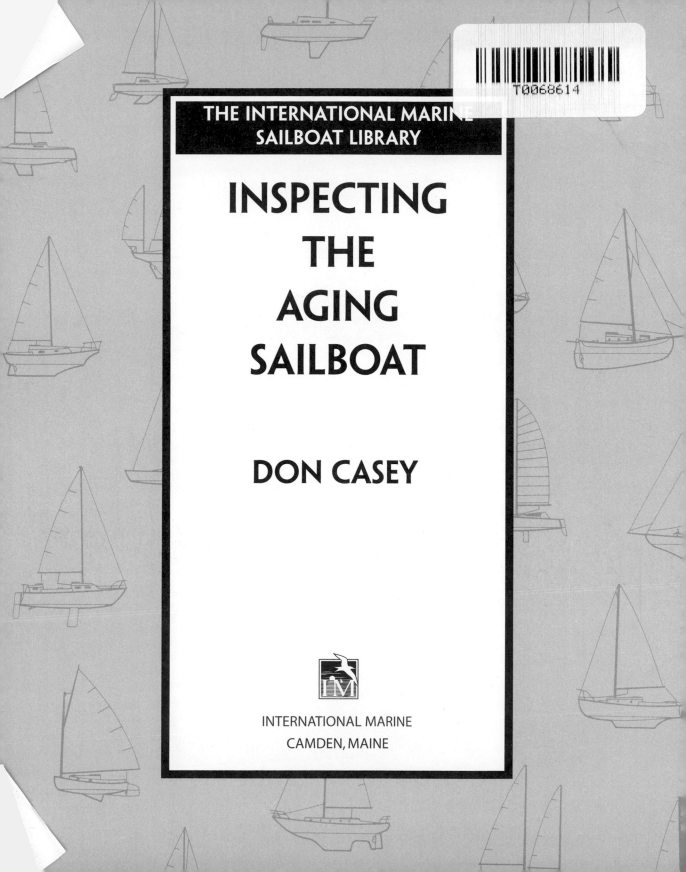

INTERNATIONAL MARINE

CAMDEN, MAINE

# CONTENTS

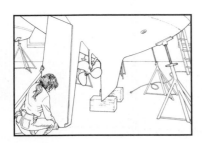 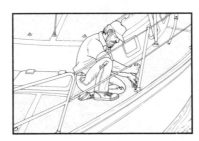 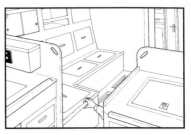

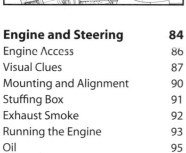

# INTRODUCTION

There are a few well-cared-for yachts into their second century of service, but most boats built 100 years ago, or even 50 years ago, are long gone—a pile of gray ash in the bottom of a boatyard stove or a punky skeleton buried in the mud of some creek or canal. Neglect is fatal to wooden boats.

In noticeable contrast, almost every sailboat larger than a skiff and built in the last 35 years, unless lost to violent weather or navigational mishap, is still around. Most see regular service. Even those sitting dirt-covered along the back fence of a boatyard are rarely beyond redemption. The reason for this new immortality is a change in the construction material.

In the late 1940s a handful of boat manufacturers abandoned the practice of constructing hulls from wood in favor of molding hulls from a war-developed synthetic polymer, reinforcing this plastic with glass fibers. Within a dozen years, virtually all production boats were being constructed of glass-reinforced plastic. Because the word "plastic" had become synonymous in 1950s America with "cheap and inferior," boat manufacturers sought to avoid this taint by calling their new construction material "fiberglass."

Plastic boats were cheaper, mostly because simplified construction techniques allowed for mass production. This made boat ownership affordable for millions who were previously excluded. As for being inferior, the ability of plastic boats to tolerate slipshod maintenance soon became legendary. Whether the addition of millions of undistinguished and poorly maintained boats to the shorelines and waterways

represented a social good is certainly debatable, but for the individual, cheaper and more durable boats were surely better.

Fiberglass boats aren't completely impervious to neglect, and they can be damaged. Moreover, a boat is more than simply a hull; many of the assembled components offer less durability. Wood used to reinforce and stiffen is subject to rot. Metal parts corrode or fatigue. Fabrics tear and mildew. Machinery wears out. While these conditions are rarely fatal—a fiberglass boat in almost any condition can be restored—the issue is value. Is making needed repairs economically sound? The answer to this question will vary according to who is considering it. A boat that should be avoided by an owner who leaves all repairs to the yard could be a bargain for the skilled do-it-yourselfer.

## SURVEYING A BOAT FOR PURCHASE

There aren't many experiences more ripe with promise than buying a boat. When you find the very craft you have been dreaming about sulking impatiently on a cradle or shifting restlessly in a slip, perfect days on the water suddenly play through your mind. You step aboard and run your fingers over her in a lover's caress. Look how perfect she is. This is the one! You stand at the helm, gripping the wheel, feeling the wind through your hair, the sun on your back, the motion of . . .

SNAP OUT OF IT!

Are those cracks in the gelcoat? Should the deck crackle like that? Are those rivets in the rubrail, and why are they loose? Why doesn't the head door close? Why are there brown streaks beneath the portlights? Are those water marks inside the galley cabinets? Should there be rust on the keel bolts? What is that bulge in the hull?

If any of these indicate real trouble (and some of them do), it is about to become your trouble. It is going to be your money paying for the repair or, God forbid, your feet treading water. So be still your beating heart; shopping for a boat is about looking for the warts.

But where do you look? And what do you look for? And when you find something, how do you know what it means? That's what this book is all about.

Wait a minute. Isn't finding a boat's problems the job of the surveyor, a real surveyor? Absolutely. If your dream boat is going to cost a substantial (by your definition) amount, a professional survey is essential. A seller is far more likely to make financial concessions based on the findings of a formal survey than on your whining about the very same things. If you plan to finance or insure the boat, a survey will be required anyway. And an experienced surveyor brings a depth of knowledge that is likely to result in findings you might overlook. So why would you want to bother with any of this if you're going to hire a pro?

Consider this. The cost to have a boat professionally surveyed runs about $10 to $15 per foot, plus travel and expenses. Haulout costs can add $3 or $4 per foot, and if you want an engine evaluated, tack on another $300 or more. You want to invest this much money only once in a boat you don't yet own, meaning that before you commission a survey, you want to be 99 percent certain that it isn't going to reveal any defects serious enough to send you looking for a different boat.

If you don't plan to hire a surveyor—a common course of action where the cost of the boat is relatively low—then you need to be 100 percent sure of the boat's condition. In either case, if you are shopping for a boat, you need to be able to look at the various candidates with a critical eye and understand the implications of what you see.

## DETERMINING THE NEEDS OF YOUR OWN BOAT

That a potential buyer needs to carefully determine a boat's overall condition is obvious, but why would an owner want to survey his or her own boat? The most important reason is safety. A single cracked wire terminal can drop the rig in a heartbeat. Unbacked cleats under load can tear free of the deck and whip through the air with potentially deadly consequences. Serious delamination reduces actual hull strength to a fraction of what is required. Chafed wire insulation can leave you treading water while your boat burns to the waterline.

The second reason is economy. Backing up cleats is sure to be cheaper than salvaging a boat released from her mooring in a blow. Caulking stanchion bases is cheaper than the major surgery of deck-core replacement. A single terminal fitting is a fraction of the cost of a whole new rig. By replacing a corroded through-hull, you could avoid rebuilding a submerged engine.

The third reason is pride. Part of the reward of owning a boat is keeping her in nice condition. An essential part of this is recognizing problems and understanding their ramifications. Most boatowners keep a weather eye open for anything irregular, but boat problems are often hidden from casual view until they become obvious in some spectacular or disheartening way. Periodic stem-to-stern surveys can reveal attention-needing conditions well before they get out of hand.

Catching potential problems early, before they have a chance to work their mischief, requires a thorough and focused examination and a discerning eye. There is nothing particularly difficult about assessing the condition of a boat; it is an essential skill for every boatowner, though too often neglected. In the pages that follow, you will learn where to look and what to look for. Take the time to develop this skill and you will save money, the occasional skipped heartbeat, and perhaps even disaster.

# HULL

The hull is the most important component of any boat. It keeps the water out and the boat afloat, and it provides the foundation for all other components. A condemned mast, engine, or deck can be replaced, but a condemned hull dooms the boat. Always start your survey with the hull.

A fair number of wood hulls are still around, but the number gets smaller every year. While well-cared-for wood hulls are remarkably long lived, such care is sadly rare. An aging wood hull is infinitely more likely to have serious problems than one constructed of fiberglass. Effectively surveying a wood hull requires specialized techniques not covered here, but some guidance in probing wood for rot can be found in "Interior."

Metal is primarily a custom boat material in the United States, but a number of European production boats have been constructed of steel or aluminum. The main risk with metal hulls is corrosion. Determining their condition essentially requires examining every square inch for telltale signs—pitting and scaling, bubbled paint, or a powdery coating. A surveyor will bang suspicious spots vigorously with a hammer.

Fiberglass is the construction material of virtually all production sailboats built in the United States. If you own a sailboat or are looking to buy one less than 35 years old, there is an overwhelming likelihood that the boat's hull will be fiberglass. Unlike wood or metal, the troubles found in fiberglass hulls are rarely natural decomposition. More often they stem from poor construction techniques or impact damage.

Determining with a high degree of certainty the condition of a fiberglass hull requires little more than good observation skills and a basic understanding of the conditions you're looking for. Laboratory tests to determine the internal condition of the laminate are rarely employed, even by professional surveyors, because they rarely reveal conditions inconsistent with the surveyor's field observations.

Look, listen, and wonder. Sharp eyes, sensitive ears, and a deductive mind are the most important tools in the fiberglass-boat surveyor's kit.

Fair means smooth and regular—without humps or flat spots. True means accurately shaped—true to her designed lines. Both are good indicators of quality and may also reveal repairs.

## HULL SIDES

Standing at the stern, position your eye near the hull, then slowly move sideways so you see more and more of the hull. Concentrate on the "horizon" of the hull, watching for it to jump or dip instead of move away smoothly. Glossy hulls are more revealing; wet the hull if it is dull, but don't confuse waves in the layer of water with irregularities in the hull. A flexible batten can help you position a flaw precisely.

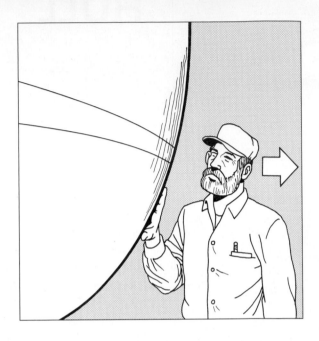

**Hardspots.** Hardspots reveal themselves as bumps or ridges in the hull. Inside the boat you will generally find a bulkhead or other structural member at the hardspot. The hardspot is caused by the hull flexing over the rigid member. Most boats reveal hardspots to the observant eye, but if the bump is pronounced, the hinging may have broken the glass fibers. Suspect some weakening of the hull.

**Flat spots.** Because thin fiberglass depends upon curvature to make it stiff, designed flat areas of the hull will be thicker and/or stiffened to compensate. Flat spots in the curved parts of a hull indicate trouble. They occasionally occur because the manufacturer removed the hull from the mold too soon, but more often they indicate weakness, damage, or a poorly executed repair. Rigging tension can dimple a flimsy hull around the chainplate attachment points. A weak hull may permanently deflect if stored in a cradle or supported by screw stands for a long time. Any impact that flattens the hull has broken or delaminated the fiberglass. Amateur repairs often "bridge" a hole rather than matching the original contour of the hull. All of these require corrective measures.

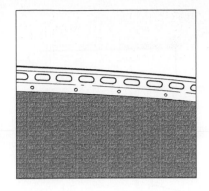

**Print-through.** Often the weave of the underlying fabric is visible in the surface of the hull, especially if the gelcoat still has its gloss. Dark colors show print-through more. A light print-through is probably not serious, but anything more than that suggests poor layup technique. Hull construction begins with a layer of gelcoat sprayed into the polished mold, then one or two layers of chopped-strand mat (CSM) begins the laminate schedule. Mat is important because it is the most watertight fabric and it provides the best foundation for a strong gelcoat bond. That it also yields the smoothest surface is an ancillary benefit, so if you see significant print-through, the manufacturer failed to put sufficient mat between the woven fabric and the gelcoat. Premature gelcoat failure is a likely consequence.

## LINES

Walk (or row) away from the hull, then circle it slowly, looking at the shape of the hull.

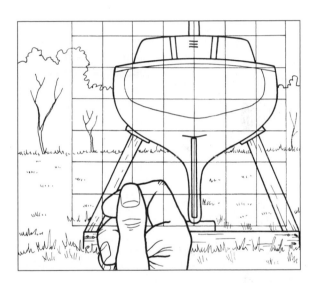

**Symmetry.** From directly forward and astern, the hull should appear symmetrical and the keel perpendicular to the deck. Sighting the hull through the gridwork of a plastic plotter simplifies this determination. Any detectable difference from one side to the other suggests major trouble.

**Distortion.** From either side, look for any change in the flow of the sheer. Overtight stays can permanently distort the hull, revealed by a break in the sheerline, usually at the mast station. Improper support during storage can also cause permanent hull distortion.

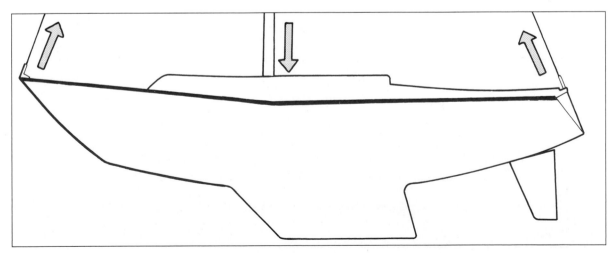

# SCANTLINGS

Older fiberglass hulls are generally of consistent thickness, but hulls built in the last 15 years are likely to be thinner above the waterline than below. This lowers costs and may improve performance, but it makes a weaker hull. Current models may be more than 1 inch thick near the keel and less than ¼ that at the rail. Whether or not the loss in strength matters depends on how the boat will be used.

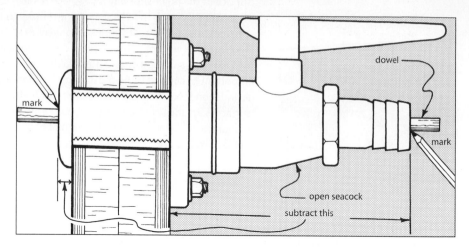

Without special equipment, you need a hole in the hull to determine its thickness. Any through-bolted hardware on the hull provides an opportunity to observe the hull thickness because you can extract a bolt. You can measure the thickness at through-hull fittings by dismantling just the hose connection. Hulls sometimes have extra thickness at through-hull locations, but you should be able to determine this by examining the inside of the hull around the through-hull. Except in extreme cases, determining the hull thickness has limited absolute value, but comparative hull thicknesses can be useful in evaluating boats from different manufacturers.

## HULL IDENTIFICATION NUMBER

SINCE 1972 BOAT MANUFACTURERS have been required to mold a 12-character hull identification number (HIN) into the transom. The prescribed code is easy to decipher. It generally looks something like this: PEA74155L485.

The first three characters are the manufacturer, the next five the model designation and the production number in the series. In this case the boat is a Pearson, coded model 74, and it is number 155 in the series. It could be the 155th boat built, but manufacturers sometimes begin a series with 100 or some other number.

Of course it's likely you already know what kind of boat you're looking at, so it is the last four numbers that are most useful. The first two are the month and year this particular model was certified by the Coast Guard. Month designations are A (January) through L (December). Year designations are 0 through 9; you have to guess the decade. The last two numbers are the model year of the boat. Keep in mind that model year often runs from August through July rather than January through December. So the HIN ending with L485 tells you that this particular model was certified in December of 1984 or, judging from the hull number (155), more likely 1974 and that it was built in 1984 or 1985. The molded-in model year can confirm or refute representations made by the seller, and the year of certification gives you a clue to the success of this particular design. TIP: New boats tend to reveal design flaws that result in some redesign, so most models are better after a year or two in production.

Sometimes manufacturers don't follow the prescribed code exactly. If you can't figure it out, call the manufacturer.

Fiberglass generally reveals stress problems with cracks in the gelcoat. The cracks can be very fine and hard to see; get close to the hull and lay your finger against the spot you are examining to ensure that your eyes focus properly. A dye penetrant such as Spot Check (available from auto-parts suppliers) can highlight hairline cracks.

Don't confuse stress cracks with surface crazing; crazing is a random pattern of cracks—something like the tapped shell of a boiled egg just before you peel it—that occurs over large areas of the boat. Stress cracks are localized and generally have an identifiable pattern to the discerning eye.

## IMPACT DAMAGE

A collision serious enough to damage the hull usually leaves a scar, but sometimes the only visible record of the event is a pattern of concentric cracks in the gelcoat. Impact with a sharp object, like the corner of a dock, leaves a bull's-eye pattern. Impact with a flat object, like a piling or a seawall, tends to put the stressed area in parentheses. Tap the hull with a plastic mallet or a screw-driver handle in the area of the impact and listen for any dull-sounding areas, which indicate delamination. Examine the hull inside for signs that the impact fractured the glass.

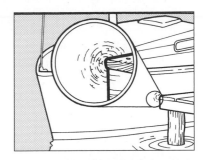

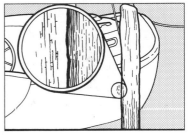

## PANTING

Panting occurs when poorly supported sections of the hull flex as the boat drives through the waves. This problem is also called oilcanning, taking its name from the domed bottom you push in and let spring back on a small oilcan. Panting usually occurs in relatively flat areas of the hull near the bow, but it may also occur in flat bilge areas and unreinforced quarters. The classic sign is a series of near-parallel cracks, sometimes crescent shaped, in the gelcoat. If you can move any portion of the hull by pushing on it, the hull lacks adequate stiffness. Left unchecked, panting can result in fatigue damage to the laminate and eventually a hinge crack all the way through the hull.

## TRANSVERSE DAMAGE

An impact on one side of a boat often results in damage to the opposite side as the force is transferred by some rigid member or just by the box effect—push on one corner of a box and all corners are distorted. Because hulls are designed to resist outside assault, the damage to the nonimpacted side—where the stress is applied from inside the hull—is often greater than to the impacted side. When you find any evidence of impact damage, always check the opposite side of the boat for collateral damage.

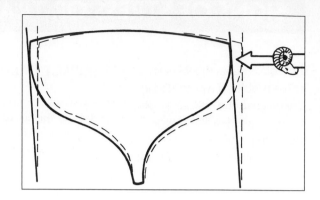

## WEEPING

Any spot on the hull that remains damp more than a few hours after the boat is hauled indicates water has penetrated the surface of the hull. Scrape away paint and you are likely to find a crack that requires repair. Weeping from an encapsulated keel can indicate a serious problem if the ballast is iron; water incursion causes the iron to rust and swell, distorting and even bursting the fiberglass. Examine the bottom of the keel and the rudder most carefully for signs of weeping.

## REPAIRS

Done well, a repair is almost impossible to detect, but this is not a concern because a proper repair will be just as strong as the original laminate. Inferior repairs are generally easier to detect. We have already mentioned flat spots. Also look for variations in the color and texture of the hull surface. It is hard to match gelcoat exactly, and careful observation will usually reveal any patching. Gelcoat paste used in a repair can also develop a porous look compared to the billiard-ball smoothness of the original gelcoat. If the hull has been painted, look for a crescent-shaped ridge that will mark a less-than-perfectly-sanded patch.

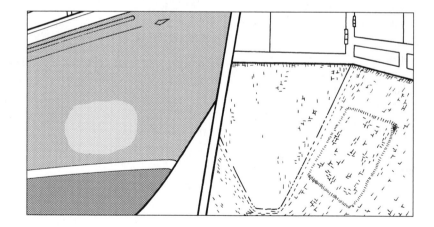

Repairs are more visible inside the hull. Any signs of lifting around the edge of a patch suggests grinding—essential for a strong repair—was inadequate. The repair shouldn't be trusted. Where you find evidence of a repair, sound the hull in a regular pattern over the entire repair area to detect voids or delamination.

# DELAMINATION

Delamination in fiberglass is the functional equivalent of rot in a wooden boat. Well-constructed solid-fiberglass hulls (meaning not cored) almost never delaminate unless they have suffered impact damage or unless water has penetrated the gelcoat (see the next section). This is because proper hull-construction technique—adding each layer before the previous one has cured—results in the resin linking chemically into a solid mass. Occasionally a manufacturer defeats this by leaving an uncompleted hull in the mold over a weekend; but most know—and do—better.

Introduce core into the formula and the likelihood of delamination increases dramatically. A core divides the hull into three distinct layers—the outer skin, the core, and the inner skin—with the bond between them strictly mechanical. Polyester resin adheres chemically to itself with amazing tenacity, but it has never been very good at adhering to other materials. At the slightest provocation it will release its grip on the core material, regardless of what it is.

## PERCUSSION TESTING

Tapping a fiberglass hull is akin to spiking a wooden one. Use a plastic mallet or the handle of a screwdriver to give the hull a light rap. If the laminate is healthy, you will get a sharp report. If it is delaminated, the sound will be a dull thud. Your hull is sure to play more than two notes, but map all suspect returns; then check inside the hull to see if a bulkhead, tank, or bag of sail is responsible. If not, it is the laminate.

It is essential to do a thorough evaluation of a cored hull because core delamination is unfortunately common and robs the hull of much of its designed strength. Tap every 2 or 3 inches over the entire surface of the hull. Be especially suspicious of the area around through-hull fittings and near signs of skin damage or repair. Percussion testing can also reveal filler patches.

# GELCOAT PROBLEMS

Most gelcoat problems are cosmetic, but a few suggest underlying structural defects.

## CHALKING

Well-applied gelcoat will last a decade with little or no maintenance, perhaps twice that long if protected with a regular application of wax. Eventually the exposed surface erodes and the gelcoat loses its gloss. To determine whether the gloss can be restored, buff an inconspicuous area with rubbing compound (formulated for fiberglass). If the gloss returns before the gelcoat becomes transparent, you may get a few more years from the surface; otherwise, painting is the preferred way to restore the gloss.

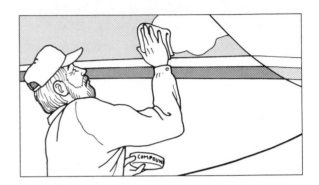

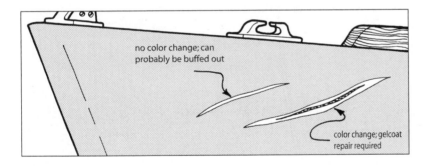

no color change; can probably be buffed out

color change; gelcoat repair required

## SCRATCHES

If scratches don't penetrate the gelcoat, they can usually be buffed out with rubbing compound. Deep scratches are easily repaired with gelcoat putty.

## CRAZING

Close examination of the gelcoat, especially on boats built in the '60s and '70s, may reveal a random egg-shell-like pattern of fine cracks which is usually caused by temperature expansion (and contraction) of the hull. It is prevalent in older boats because the gelcoat was thicker and thus less flexible. Correcting this condition requires filling the cracks with epoxy and painting the repaired surface.

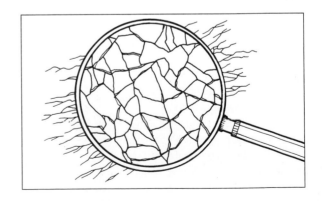

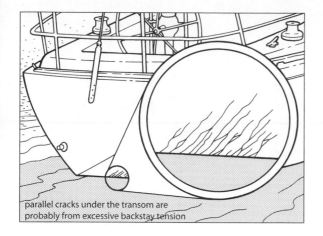

parallel cracks under the transom are probably from excessive backstay tension

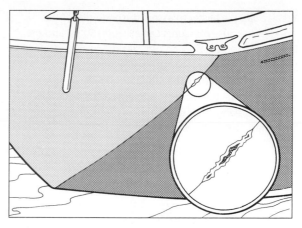

## STRESS CRACKING

Unlike crazing, stress cracks are usually localized and exhibit a discernible pattern. As previously mentioned, stress cracks can indicate impact damage or panting. They are a valuable clue for a number of other conditions detailed in this chapter. If you find cracks in the gelcoat, figure out why they are there before moving on.

## VOIDS

The reluctance of glass fabric to take a sharp bend causes it to pull away from the gelcoat on inside corners during the layup process, creating voids. On a hull, this condition is generally confined to the stem, the corners where the hull sides intersect the transom, and the turn of the hull flange. Percussion testing reveals voids and may break them open. Voids are a cosmetic flaw and easily repaired with gelcoat putty.

# BLISTERS

Blisters reveal themselves as bumps in the surface of fiberglass and are easily detected by simply examining the hull. A blister can be as small as a ladybug or as big as your hand.

## GELCOAT BLISTERS

Blisters occur because free water-soluble chemicals inside the laminate exert an osmotic pull on water outside, and some water molecules find a way through the slightly permeable gelcoat. As more water is attracted into the enclosed space, internal pressure builds. The water molecules aren't squirted back out the way they came in because they combine with the attracting chemicals into a solution with a larger molecular structure. Instead, the pressure pushes the covering gelcoat into a dome—a blister.

Break a sample blister to assess the condition. Wear goggles because pressures can exceed 150 psi and the liquid that comes spraying out is acid. Scrub out the blister with water and a brush and examine the underlying laminate. If the laminate is perfect—the usual finding—the blister is primarily a cosmetic flaw, although taking steps to prevent water from reaching the laminate may be prudent.

## LAMINATE BLISTERS

If the laminate is damaged, repairs will be more extensive, but this is still not a dangerous condition as long as the number of blisters is small. Use a knife point to find the depth of the damage. Laminate blisters most often occur between the initial layer(s) of mat and the first layer of woven roving—probably because the manufacturer was religious about getting the initial mat laid into the mold while the gelcoat was still chemically active, but was less exacting about the timing for completing the layup. Or it may be due to a failure to roll the roving sufficiently against the resin-stiffened mat to eliminate all voids. Whatever the reason, laminate blisters below the first layers of mat are no more dangerous than gelcoat blisters.

If additional layers of the laminate are involved in the blister, the area will have to be treated like any other delamination. How serious the problem is depends on the number and size of the laminate blisters.

## POX

For pox, examine the bottom as soon as it comes out of the water. In the early stages blisters can shrink and even disappear altogether. If the bottom is covered with hundreds of blisters, the boat has pox. Boat pox is a much more serious condition than a handful of blisters scattered over the bottom of a 15-year-old hull. It is a systemic condition and will only worsen unless remedial action is taken.

To cure boat pox you must grind away all the gelcoat below the waterline. Just opening and filling the blisters won't do because a hull with pox is saturated throughout and won't dry out unless the gelcoat is removed. Once the hull is dry, which can take several months, the usual process is to apply a new barrier coat of epoxy. The cost to have this done professionally is between $300 and $400 per foot of boat length. Most of this is labor, so the cost if you do it yourself is much more modest, but it is a nasty job at best.

# MOISTURE CONTENT

Floating fiberglass hulls absorb moisture, sometimes a significant amount. Water makes the boat heavier, and it puts the gelcoat and laminate at risk for blisters. The only way to determine the absolute moisture content is to cut a plug from the hull, weigh it, oven-dry it, then weigh it again. The difference in the two weights is the moisture content. But unless you have reason to believe that the laminate is saturated, this type of testing is unnecessary.

## MOISTURE METERS

Professional surveyors use moisture meters, and boatyards sometimes have a moisture meter available. These typically measure electromagnetic capacitance and convert that into percentage of moisture content. Moisture-meter readings are notoriously misleading. For example, readings as high as 25 percent are not uncommon, but the actual moisture content of saturated fiberglass laminate is unlikely to exceed 4 percent. Despite claims to the contrary, moisture meters tell you very little about the interior of the laminate. Generally you must remove the bottom paint to even get a reading from the fiberglass.

These limitations don't mean moisture-meter readings are useless. A series of moisture-meter readings can identify areas of the hull that are wet relative to other areas. And meter readings taken over time should flatten out, giving you an indication that the hull has reached its driest state. On a boat that has been out of the water for several weeks, a reading around 5 percent suggests the hull is dry.

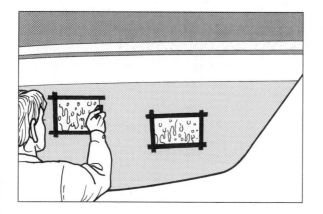

## PLASTIC

You can accomplish much the same thing with 6-inch squares of plastic freezer bag. To see if a hull is wet, tape several squares to different locations on the hull, using electrical tape and sealing all four edges. After 24 hours, check the plastic. If moisture has condensed on the interior surface, the hull is wet. This works best when the day is sunny and relatively warm.

To monitor the drying process, do this test periodically over a period of weeks or months. When the plastic remains dry even in bright sunlight, the hull is dry.

# KEEL

The occurrence of keel problems seems to be directly related to the keel's aspect ratio. The greater the chord— the keel's fore and aft dimension—the less vulnerable the keel.

## ALIGNMENT

Keels on wooden sailboats are often found to have taken a twist or cant, but fiberglass boats only rarely exhibit this condition. Occasionally manufacturers remove the hull from the mold too soon and the keel or keel pad moves before the laminate reaches full cure. A straightedge held at arm's length will let you check the keel against the mast or the horizontal plane of the deck.

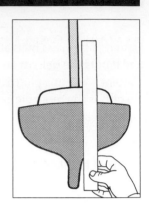

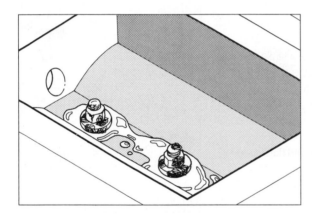

## ATTACHMENT

Quality bronze or stainless steel keel bolts can last half a century or longer, but they are susceptible to life-shortening corrosion when wet or exposed. If the keel-to-hull joint isn't completely sealed, stainless steel keel bolts are likely to develop crevice corrosion. Bilge water is more likely to be the catalyst, so manufacturers often encapsulate the tops in resin to seal them. This undoubtedly extends the lives of the bolts, but it precludes easy examination. Fortunately catastrophic keel-bolt failure on an otherwise sound fiberglass boat is highly unlikely; but to be certain you can have the keel x-rayed. If the bolts are exposed, visually check them for corrosion and signs of leakage. They should have a generous shoulder washer under the nut. For every 1,500 pounds of external ballast, the keel should have at least 1 square inch of bolt sectional area; this is called Nevin's Rule.

**Hull attachment.** When the keel is bolted directly to the hull, the bolts should pass through floor "timbers" or a reinforcing grid. Check the timbers and grid for any signs of stress cracking.

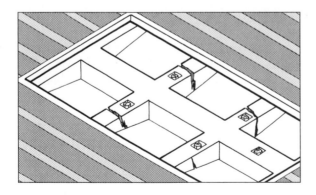

**Stub-keel attachment.** Bolting the ballast keel to a molded stub keel is generally a stronger design. Check the keel-to-stub joint for any signs of movement. Separation at the joint puts stainless steel keel bolts at risk for crevice corrosion, and their integrity will be in question unless they are inspected.

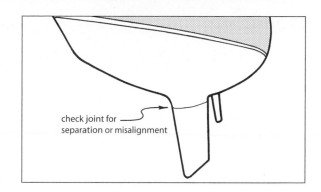

check joint for separation or misalignment

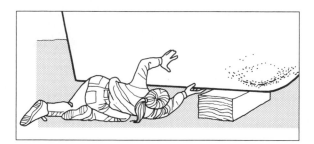

**Encapsulated ballast.** When the keel is a hollow part of the hull filled with ballast, problems are rare. Check both sides of the keel for swelling; if the ballast is iron—common in boats built outside the United States—water intrusion can cause it to rust and expand. The bottom of the keel is most damage prone, so be sure to examine it carefully. This requires having the yard lift the boat or at least reposition the keel blocks.

Also check the bilge to make sure the top of the ballast cavity is sealed. If this part of the bilge can hold standing water, set a glass in it and pour water into the bilge and the glass to the same level. Check in a couple of days; if the level of the bilge water is lower than the level of the water in the glass, the bilge is leaking into the keel cavity.

If you suspect water intrusion, drill a couple of exploratory holes through or near the bottom of the keel. Use only a hand drill or a battery-operated drill for this. If there is water in the cavity, the holes will serve as drains, and they also allow you to determine the ballast material. Find and repair the leaks into the cavity, then repair the drilled holes with epoxy laminate (see *Sailboat Hull and Deck Repair* in this series).

## GROUNDING

Going aground in mud or sand is usually harmless, but striking rock or coral while under way subjects the hull to a pile-driver-like blow. When the impact is to the lowest part of the keel, the lever effect multiplies the already considerable forces and concentrates them. Any signs of damage to the front or the bottom of the keel should have you carefully examining the area where the keel joins the hull. A bump in front of the keel or a dimple behind it suggests serious damage. Remove the bottom paint to check for cracks. Also examine these areas from inside the hull.

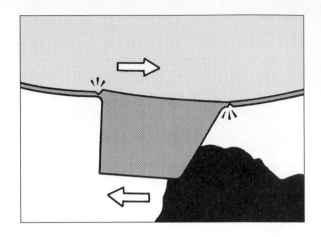

## CENTERBOARDS

Except in lightly built racers, fiberglass construction has eliminated most of the problems that traditionally plagued wooden centerboarders—except fouling—but there are a few conditions to be on the lookout for.

**Board.** Check metal centerboards with a straightedge to make sure they have not been bent by grounding. A bent centerboard can usually be pressed or hammered back into true. Fiberglass centerboards are constructed much like rudders and should be inspected as detailed in the rudder section on page 24.

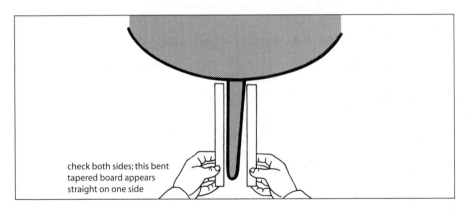

check both sides; this bent tapered board appears straight on one side

**Trunk.** The monocoque construction made possible by fiberglass usually yields a strong and leak-free centerboard trunk. The case is typically an integral, molded feature of the hull and should be examined in the same manner as the rest of the hull. In a keel/centerboard configuration where the centerboard is entirely housed within the ballast keel, the likelihood of leakage or structural problems is low. To inspect the interior of the case, the boat must be hoisted enough for the board to be fully lowered.

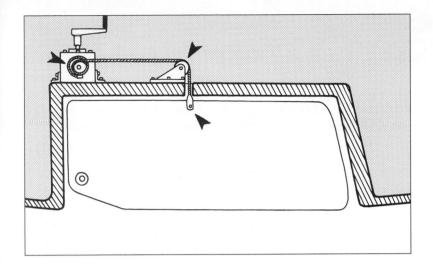

**Pendant.** Inspect the wire pendant for rust and broken strands. Look for wear on the fitting that lets the pendant into the boat. If the pendant runs in a groove over the top of the centerboard, look for marks outside the groove that might suggest that the pendant is slipping out of the groove, which risks jamming the board.

**Pivot pin.** Check the pivot pin (or the hole) for wear by trying to move the lowered board up and down or fore and aft. The pivot pin on most centerboard boats is essentially a shoulder bolt passing through both sides of the trunk. Check the grommets on either end for resilience and for signs of leakage.

The pin on a keel/centerboard is usually inaccessible, captured by resin plugs on either side. It can be the source of leakage into the ballast cavity, indicated by weeping around the pin (inside the trunk) after the boat has otherwise dried out. If the pin isn't loose or weeping, it generally requires no further attention, although stainless steel pins are subject to crevice corrosion. Determining the condition of the pin requires extraction.

# RUDDER

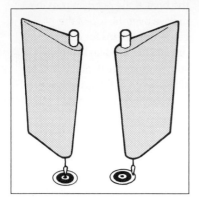

A sailboat rudder should have nearly neutral buoyancy so it neither floats nor sinks when the boat heels. Wood satisfies this requirement, and some early fiberglass sailboats had wood rudders, but most sailboat rudders are foam-filled or hollow fiberglass constructions.

## SPADE RUDDERS

Spade rudders are built around the lower end of a length of tube or bar stock, with the tiller or steering quadrant attached to the upper end. The stock both turns the rudder and attaches it to the boat.

**1** Check the vertical alignment of the rudder (above). Observe the bottom of the rudder blade as someone else moves the tiller or wheel from hard over to hard over. If the stock is bent it will be obvious.

**2** Tie or lock the tiller or wheel, then try to turn the blade. If it moves, the internal structure of the rudder is broken or the filler has deteriorated, and the rudder will have to be rebuilt.

**3** Examine the rudder port—where the stock enters the hull—and the hull around it. If the rudder comes under the strain of grounding or catching a line, will the stock bend or will it pry a hole in the bottom of the boat? A strong rudder installation requires reinforcement of the rudder tube well above the hull.

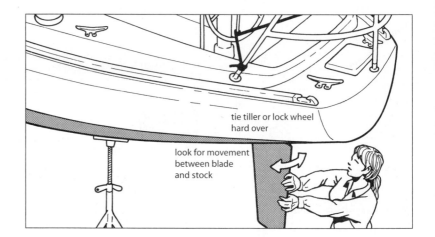

tie tiller or lock wheel hard over

look for movement between blade and stock

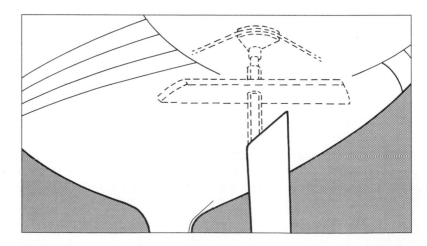

## KEEL-HUNG

Hinging the rudder to the aft end of the keel provides fewer opportunities for rudder damage but is only possible with a keel that runs well aft.

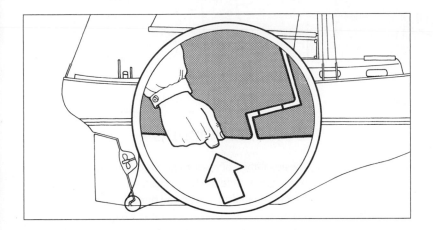

**1** Shake the rudder blade at the bottom. Some play in the heel fitting is acceptable, but the socket shouldn't be elongated or the pin obviously worn.

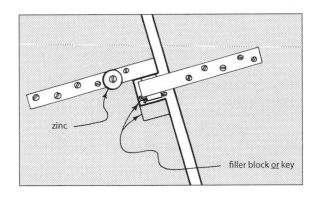

zinc

filler block <u>or</u> key

**2** If the rudder hinges on pintles and gudgeons, check them for wear. Also check to make sure they are well mounted to both the hull and the rudder. They should have keys or filler blocks to prevent them from coming unshipped, and generally they should be protected with zinc anodes.

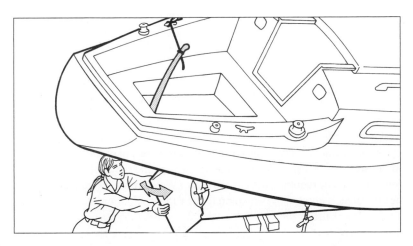

**3** Check the rudder/stock attachment by locking the steering and trying to turn the blade.

## SKEG-MOUNTED

To gain some of the advantages of a keel mounting without the disadvantages of a long keel, rudders are often attached to a leading skeg. Check a skeg-mounted rudder exactly as one hinged to the keel. In addition, examine the skeg carefully, paying particular attention to its alignment and its attachment to the hull.

## OUTBOARD RUDDERS

The advantage of an outboard rudder is that the stock doesn't penetrate the hull. In fact, there is no stock; the tiller (or quadrant) is attached directly to the blade. The rudder is, however, vulnerable to collision from the rear. Examine the aft edge of the rudder, and check the pintles and gudgeons.

## CONSTRUCTION

Occasionally rudders are constructed by wrapping fiberglass cloth around the core, but more often they are molded in two shell-like halves, then bonded together around the stock and the core.

**Water intrusion.** Rudder skins are typically thin, making the rudder relatively fragile. Examine the rudder (and the centerboard) carefully for cracks or weeping. Pay particular attention to the bottom of the rudder and to the area where the rudderstock passes through the skin. Inspection of the latter usually requiring the aid of a mirror. Water inside the rudder alters its buoyancy, is potentially damaging to the rudder's interior framework, and is a freeze risk in winter.

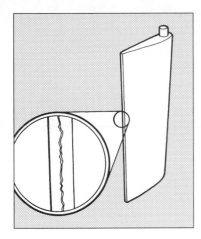

**Center split.** The joint between the two halves of molded rudder blades fails regularly. Examine every inch of the joint for signs of separation.

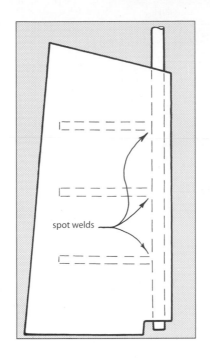

spot welds

**Broken framework.** With the tiller or wheel locked, if you can move the rudder, the interior framework is probably broken. Too often the internal framework is little more than two or three metal straps or rods spot-welded to the stock. When these welds break, the rudder rotates on the stock. Any movement of the rudder on the stock means the rudder must be cut apart and rebuilt.

# CUTLESS BEARING AND PROPELLER

The Cutless bearing provides a bearing surface for the shaft where it exits the hull. Cutless bearings are generally a splined rubber tube inside a bronze housing.

**1** Try to move the shaft side-to-side and up-and-down. Some play is normal, but if the shaft rattles, the Cutless bearing is worn and needs replacing.

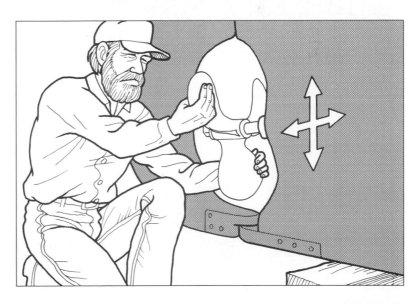

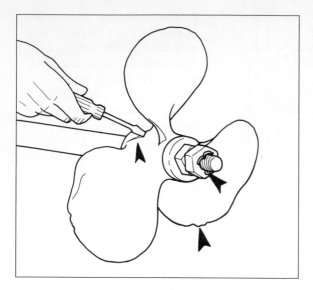

**2** Examine the prop for nicks, corrosion, and bent blades. Scratch the hub to check the prop for galvanic corrosion: yellow is good, pink is bad. Look at the condition of the threads at the end of the shaft, and make sure the retaining nuts are tight and secured with a cotter pin.

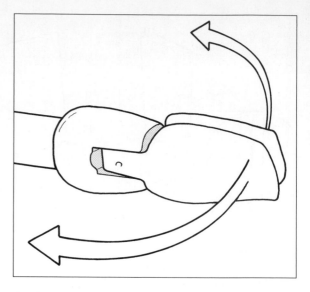

**3** If the prop is supposed to feather or fold, make sure it operates smoothly.

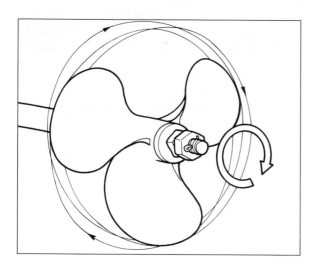

**4** Rotate the prop to check the shaft for any bend.

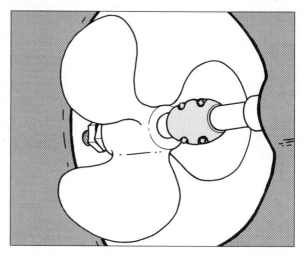

**5** The shaft should have a zinc collar in good condition (even if electrically isolated with a rubber coupling). The zinc should not be against the Cutless bearing or it will restrict the lubricating flow of water to the bearing.

# THROUGH-HULL FITTINGS

Through-hull fittings are not very complicated—nothing more than a threaded pipe with an integral flange on one side, a clamping nut on the other.

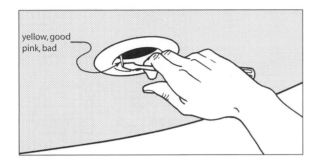

yellow, good
pink, bad

## BRONZE

A patina on bronze skin fittings usually indicates nothing more than surface tarnish. Scratch the bronze with the corner of a screwdriver; if the exposed metal has a pinkish hue, the zinc has leeched out of the bronze and the remaining alloy is probably brittle. The fitting should be replaced.

## PLASTIC

Early plastic through-hulls were brittle and dangerous, but the best modern ones are made of glass-reinforced resin (Marelon)—much like the hull they are usually installed in. Their biggest advantage is that they are not subject to corrosion. Some sailors object to plastic through-hulls below the waterline, but there is no evidence that Marelon through-hulls fail more often than bronze ones. It is unlikely that many of the old brittle through-hulls are still around, but unfortunately cheap plastic skin fittings intended for topside use are still available. Give all plastic fittings a good rap with a plastic mallet to check them. Make sure that only plastic nuts and plastic seacocks are used on plastic through-hulls; never mix bronze and plastic.

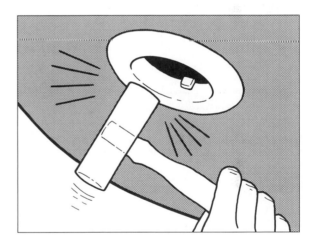

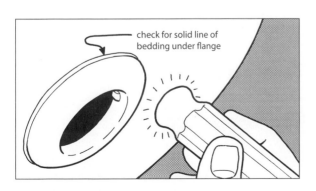

check for solid line of bedding under flange

## BEDDING

Check all around the through-hull flange for a continuous bead of bedding. If there is any indication that the seal has broken, the edges of the laminate around the hole may be exposed to water. The through-hull should be removed, cleaned, and rebedded in polyurethane sealant. Tap the hull around all skin fittings for evidence of delamination.

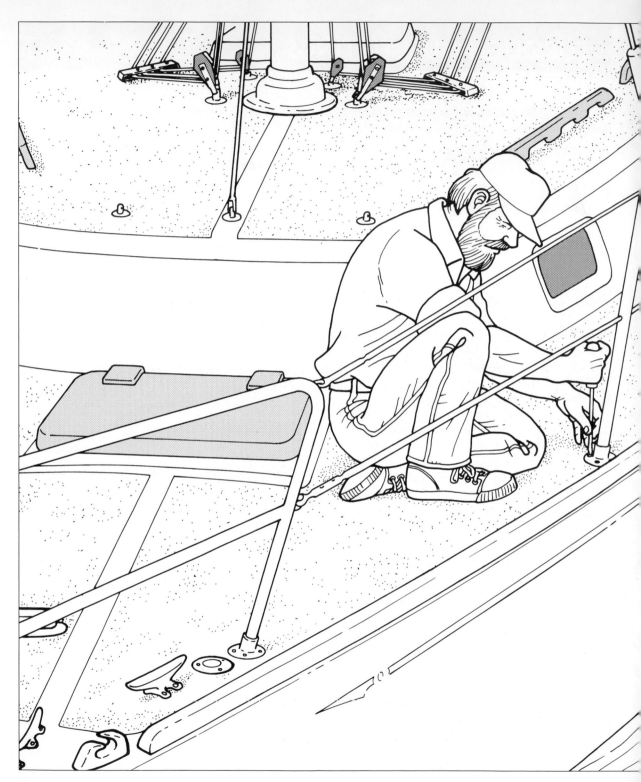

# DECK

Unless you are terribly ham-fisted at the helm, it is the deck that sustains the worst treatment. You walk on it, carefully perhaps when the boat was new, but later with no more concern than you give a concrete sidewalk. It lies horizontal beneath the sun, like a staked-out Foreign Legionnaire. It is coated with salt, assaulted by acid rain. The freeze-thaw-freeze cycle of winter moisture in crevices and cracks, like clicks of a jack, pry the deck apart.

To endure, a deck needs to be strong, but weight carried high in a boat reduces stability, so first it needs to be light. Heavy abuse and light construction—not a combination that suggests longevity. In addition, decks are usually landscapes of corners, angles, and textures, each introducing new problems into the equation.

Glass-reinforced plastic is inherently flexible, but most of us want the deck to be stiff, to feel solid underfoot. Stiffening the deck without adding excessive weight requires cored construction—with all the potential problems that implies. You can shy away from a cored hull, but limiting yourself to boats without cored deck makes for extremely slim pickings.

Despite this, more deck problems (excluding the hull-to-deck joint) are the result of poor care and maintenance than of poor design and construction. Leaving the deck uncovered through the winter is murder on the laminate. Failure to properly bed deck hardware is a death warrant for the core.

Deck repairs are likely to be more costly and/or time consuming than comparable hull repairs. The angles and textures complicate laminate repair. Core is more likely to be involved. The deck is laden with a wide array of hardware which may have to be removed. And access to the underside of the deck is almost certain to be restricted.

Identifying deck problems early and taking the appropriate corrective action can prevent more serious damage. You should carefully survey the deck of your own boat at least once a year.

# HULL-TO-DECK JOINT

Perhaps the very best clue to the overall construction of a boat is the hull-to-deck joint. Conscientious manufacturers make sure these joints are strong and will remain watertight long after the warranty expires.

Hull-to-deck joints generally fall into one of three categories, each with advantages and drawbacks. Identifying the type your boat has will make examination easier.

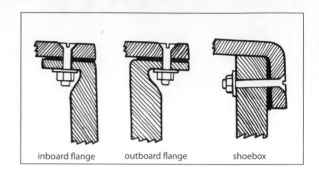

inboard flange     outboard flange     shoebox

## CHECKING THE JOINT

**1** From inside look for any signs of past leakage—discoloration, dust rivulets, etc. Much of the joint may be inaccessible, but sample segments may be observed from the forepeak and the cockpit lockers.

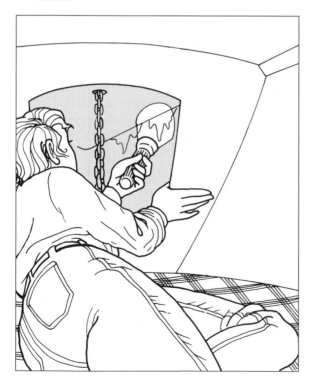

**2** From outside, be suspicious if you see a fillet of caulk along either edge of the rail.

**3** To fully inspect the joint, remove the covering rail or molding.

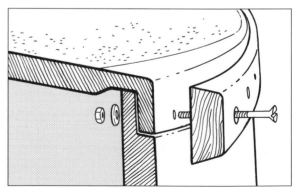

# FASTENING

**1** Pop rivets are soft by design and a poor way to join the deck to the hull. The pulsating stresses on the joint eventually stretch the rivet and allow the joint to loosen.

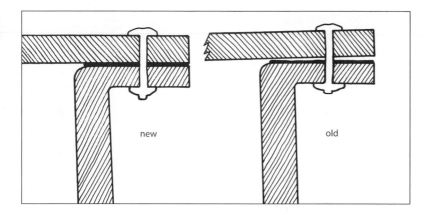

new                    old

**2** Self-tapping screws are better than pop rivets, but the strength of the joint is limited to the grip the threads have on the laminate. This is likely to be inadequate in rough seas or any kind of collision.

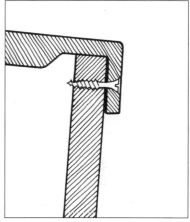

**3** The best joints are fastened together with stainless steel bolts on about 6-inch centers. Wider spacing can allow the joint to separate between fasteners. Manufacturers sometimes let the toerail or rubrail bolts serve double duty—perfectly acceptable.

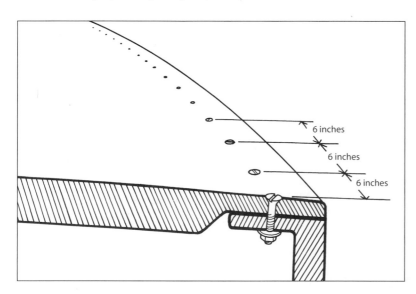

6 inches

6 inches

6 inches

## TRACKING A LEAK

LEAKS DON'T ALWAYS leave a trail behind, but you can set a trap for the sneaky ones. Using a washable marker, simply draw a horizontal line high on the interior of the hull everywhere you have access. After the next hard rainstorm or wet beat to weather, inspect the line. Leaks will be flagged with a blurry break in the line and probably a streak of color down the hull. You can wash off the marker after your test, or leave it as an active monitoring system.

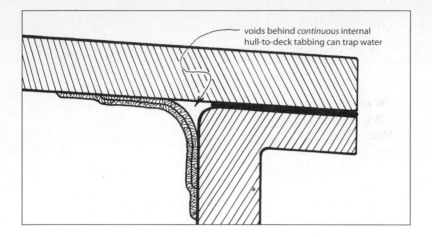

voids behind *continuous* internal hull-to-deck tabbing can trap water

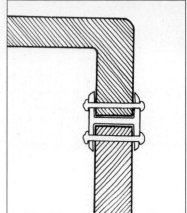

**4** A few manufacturers have strengthened the joint by tabbing the hull and deck together with fiberglass. This generally makes a strong, watertight joint, but be sure it has not been done in such a way that it causes the joint to trap water, especially if the boat will be subjected to freezing temperatures.

**5** Occasionally you may come across an older boat with the hull and deck joined by an H-shaped extrusion. This has proven to be a very poor method and should be avoided.

## SEALANT

With the rail or molding removed, check to make sure the joint is fully caulked and the sealant still supple. Petroleum-based sealants eventually harden; the proper sealant for the hull-to-deck joint is polyurethane. A night inspection with a helper shining a bright light on the joint inside the boat can reveal otherwise undetectable separations.

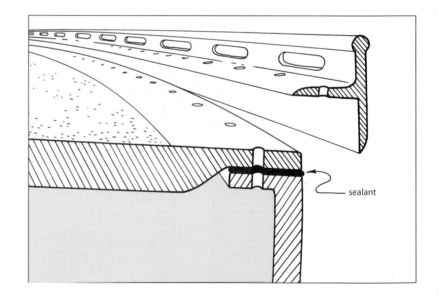

sealant

# SURFACE DAMAGE

The gelcoat surface of the deck almost always has a shorter life than that of the hull. Some well-meaning manufacturers tried to compensate for this by making the deck gelcoat thicker, but this generally made matters worse.

## CRAZING

Crazing is caused by temperature expansion and is more common on early fiberglass boats. Crazing is typically widespread, often covering most or all of the smooth deck surfaces. True crazing, i.e., not caused by flexing of the underlying laminate, is a cosmetic condition easily repaired with high-build epoxy primer.

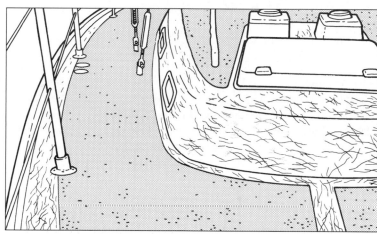

## STRESS CRACKING

Stress cracks are evidence that the deck has flexed beyond the capacity of the gelcoat. Stress cracks are usually localized, although lightly built boats sometimes exhibit stress cracks over every inch of the deck.

**Alligatoring.**  A random pattern of stress cracks over a wide area is sometimes called alligatoring. Caused by excessive flexing of the underlying laminate, it looks similar to crazing, but with a much larger pattern. Alligatoring often indicates core delamination, which destroys the deck's stiffness and allows the top skin to flex.

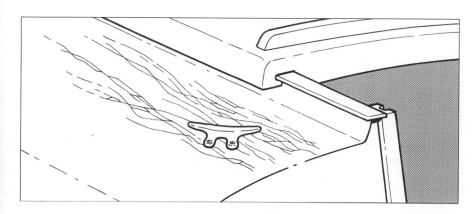

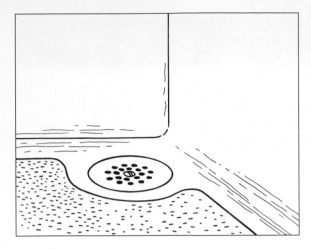

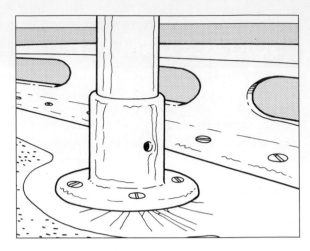

**Parallel cracks.** Hinge cracks are a common condition, caused by repeated flexing of the deck at a weak location. Look for parallel hinge cracks where the cockpit sides meet the sole and where the side decks intersect the trunk. Repairs require strengthening and/or stiffening the area.

**Star cracks.** Star cracks result from "pinpoint" stresses. The most common deck star cracks radiate from the bolt holes under stanchion bases—a direct result of the deck being levered up (or down) by force applied to the top of the stanchion. A backing plate that spreads the stresses is the usual preventative measure.

## BREAKOUT

Because of the numerous corners in a deck mold, gelcoat voids are all too common. It is not unusual to find a boat with a flawless hull and a deck as pockmarked as a rural road sign. Voids in the flat expanse of the deck suggest inferior layup technique; but if they are confined to sharp outside corners of deck features, they show only that the designer was more concerned with style than with the realities of production fiberglass layup. Deck traffic quickly breaks out sizable voids; so an older boat without open voids means either good design and layup or voids that have been repaired. Check for voids by percussion testing the deck.

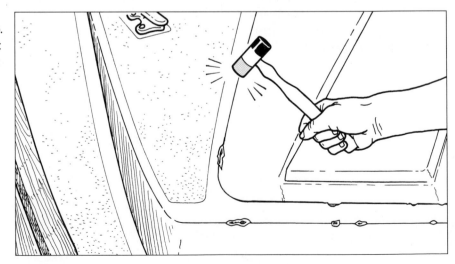

# NONSKID

Most fiberglass boats have texture molded into the deck to provide secure footing. The design challenge—met with varying success—has always been to make the texture rough enough without being uncomfortable. Over time, traffic wears away sharp edges and painting fills depressions, reducing nonskid qualities. Check the deck wet and with marginal shoes; inadequate traction is as dangerous as a weak hull.

# CORE PROBLEMS

Almost every decked fiberglass sailboat has core in the deck, usually end-grain balsa. Balsa is light and resists saturation when installed properly. Plywood is often substituted in hardware-mount areas for its higher compression strength. Relatively flat areas of the deck may be cored entirely with plywood. Plywood is stiffer and stronger, but much less resistant to saturation. Several types of plastic foam are also used as core material.

## DELAMINATION

Crackling underfoot suggests delamination. Percussion test the deck to find and map delaminated areas. A delaminated deck often exhibits humps and alligatoring.

Domestic builders have been conscientious about using only marine-grade plywood for plywood cores, but a number of imported boats were built with lesser grades. The glue in these plywoods dissolves when they get wet and the plywood delaminates, losing all structural integrity. Such decks become springy and must be totally reconstructed.

## WET CORE

Wet core can feel and sound squishy underfoot; water pumping out around deck-mounted hardware is a sure sign. Water usually enters deck core material through improperly sealed hardware mounting holes. If percussion testing reveals delamination near a piece of hardware—saturated core may sound less hollow than dry delamination, but not sharp like healthy core—remove the hardware and probe the core with a tissue-wrapped screwdriver; moisture on the tissue suggests a wet core.

Seal the mounting holes—top and bottom—with plastic, then check the plastic at the end of a sunny day; condensation inside the plastic suggests moisture in the core.

You can confirm suspected wet core by drilling into it through the top skin. If the core is saturated, the material the drill brings out will be wet.

Foam cores are generally unaffected by moisture, but wet foam is still a serious condition. The hydraulic pumping action from just walking on a saturated deck tends to hammer the skins apart, and if the boat is subject to freezing conditions, the expansion rips them apart. Regardless of core material, the space between the inner and outer deck skins must be dry.

## ROT

Balsa resists rot, but if it remains saturated for a long period, the effect is the same: the core becomes mushy and weak and separates from the sandwiching skins. Probing the core with a wire through a hole in the skin will give you a clue as to the integrity of the core material.

Plywood rots and virtually disintegrates if it is allowed to remain wet. A soft deck suggests rotten core. This is easily confirmed with a wire probe.

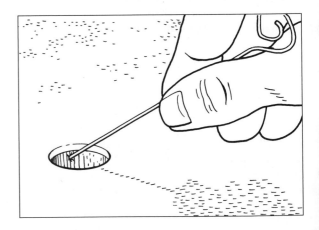

# HATCHES

Hatches must be strong and watertight. Even hatches with a high coaming need a gasket to be truly watertight. Modern hatches depend entirely on gaskets.

## DECK HATCHES

**1** Check the integrity of the hatch; wooden hatches tend to come apart if they aren't well maintained, and fiberglass hatches are sometimes so thin, especially on the sides, that they crack or split.

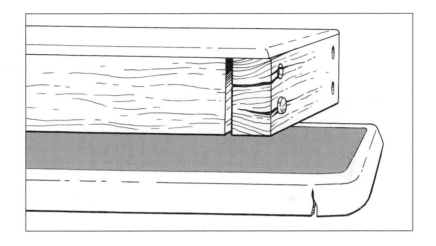

**2** Gaskets are almost invariably kept in service long past their useful life. Check the gasket to make sure it is still supple. Also inspect the hinges, support, and latch for distortion or corrosion.

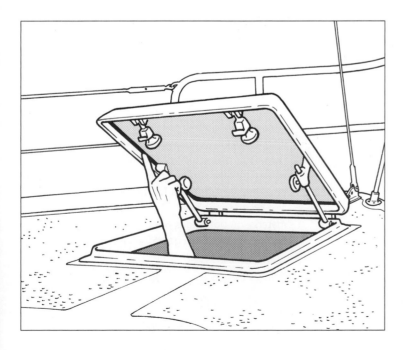

# COMPANIONWAY HATCH

**1** Carefully inspect the rabbets or notches that retain a sliding companionway hatch; hatches sometimes stress-crack in the bottom of the rabbet, and a healthy jerk will separate the hatch from the boat.

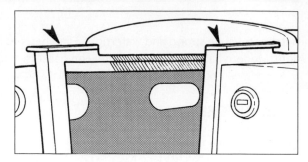

**2** For easy hatch operation, the rails should be perfectly straight. Overtight stays can cause distortion; loosen the backstay tension and check the rails again. If the beds for the rails aren't flat, fairing them with epoxy putty, then reinstalling the rails will generally cure a "sticky" hatch.

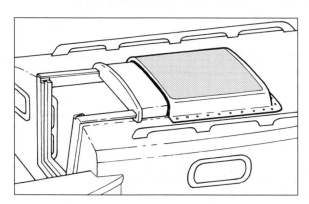

**3** Don't expect a sliding hatch to be truly watertight; a sea hood over its forward end helps. Sea hoods need to be well fastened to the deck and strong enough to stand on.

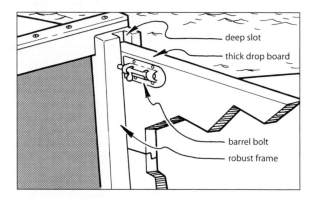

deep slot

thick drop board

barrel bolt

robust frame

**4** It may be possible to construct a companionway door as strong as dropboards, but it rarely happens. Outside of protected waters, dropboards are essential. Make sure they are thick enough to take a breaking wave. The slot for the hatch boards should also be up to the task—deep, with plenty of material on both sides. Barrel bolts to hold the boards in place are a good feature.

# COCKPIT LOCKERS

**1** The most essential concern is keeping the lid in place. Hinges are often inadequate; the fiberglass should fail before the hinge does. Make certain each hatch has a securable latch strong enough to hold if the contents of the locker fall against the inside of the lid in a knockdown.

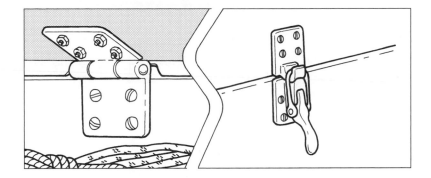

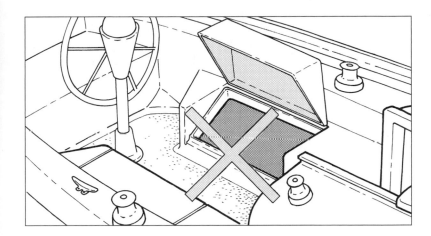

**2** Cockpit hatches rarely have a gasket, depending on deep coamings to channel the water away. Such coamings should never be low enough for cockpit flooding to flood the hatch.

## COCKPIT FLOODING

COCKPIT DESIGN IS NOT TECHNICALLY a survey issue, but that is little consolation if you strengthen hatch boards and locker latches but still end up treading water. A companionway at cockpit-sole level is dangerous, and keeping the lower board in place is a poor substitute for a bridge deck. Cockpit drains are almost always too small; they should be capable of lowering the water below the level of the hatch coamings in a matter of seconds, capable of emptying the cockpit entirely in a minute or two.

# PORTLIGHTS

Portlights must be leak free and strong enough to resist a boarding wave. If they are fixed, they should be clear, and if they are opening, they should seal with a light turn on the dogs.

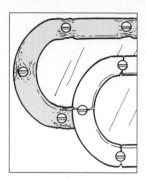

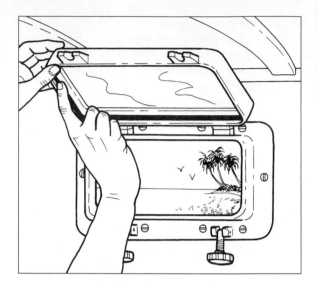

**1** Check frames for damage or distortion. Plastic frames have a poor record of durability. Aluminum frames tend to corrode, sometimes beyond use. Bronze and stainless give few problems.

**2** Check the gasket on opening ports. If it is not soft and supple, replace it. Overtightening the dogs in an effort to get a "dead" gasket to seal is the biggest cause of damage to opening ports; a couple of easy turns on the dogs should be sufficient.

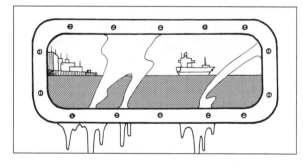

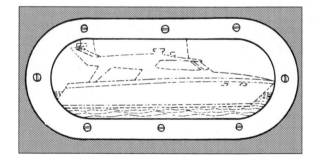

**3** Water stains beneath a deadlight suggest that the port needs to be removed and rebedded. Beneath an opening port, water stains may only reflect that the port was left open when it should have been closed.

**4** Over time plastic portlights get scratched and sometimes craze. Replacing them is not difficult if the frames are sound, and clear portlights make a big difference in both the appearance of the boat and the view from the cabin.

# DECK HARDWARE

Part of a deck survey is an examination of the hardware attached to the deck. Spars, rigging, and steering systems are covered elsewhere in this book.

## MOUNTING

Oil-discharge plaques and speed-log bevels can be mounted with screws, but virtually every other item of deck hardware should be through-bolted to the deck. All items that might come under stress—such as cleats, winches, pulpits, and stanchion bases—need a generous backing plate on the underside of the deck. Metal, preferably stainless steel, is the material of choice; wood backers tend to compress, and fiberglass laminate, unless obtrusively thick, is too flexible.

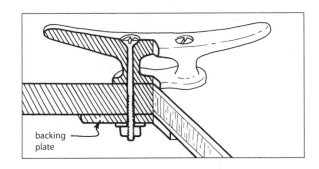

backing plate

## BEDDING

**1** Below deck, check for signs of leakage—water stains, dust rivulets, mildew, corrosion on the mounting bolts or backing plate. On deck, examine all sides of the base of each item; a properly bedded item sits on a thin "gasket" of sealant. Anywhere there is a void or the base sits hard against the deck is a potential leak. Sealant beaded or filleted around the edge of the base is a sure sign of leakage. Sealant below deck is also a sign of a leakage problem; backing plates should never be bedded.

**2** Depending on sealant to keep water out of core material is an invitation to disaster. If the hardware is installed on a cored area, remove a mounting bolt and probe the hole with wire. Top-quality boats have solid laminate in designed hardware-mount areas. If the core is exposed in the hole, the mounting holes should be drilled oversize, filled with epoxy, then redrilled for the bolts (see *Sailboat Hull and Deck Repair* in this series). Bedding is still required.

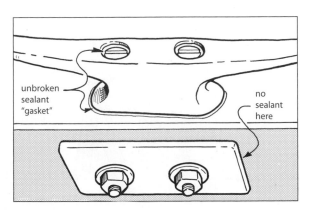

unbroken sealant "gasket"

no sealant here

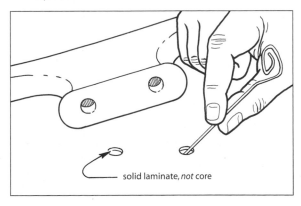

solid laminate, *not* core

## WINCHES

Turn each winch drum backward (usually counterclockwise) slowly and listen to the pawls. You should hear two distinct clicks, and both pawls should seat at each click with a solid snap. Make a complete revolution, then do it again reversing your effort at each click to make sure the pawls seat in each tooth of the gear. Insert the winch handle and turn it backward to check the spindle pawls the same way. Now spin the drum; it should spin easily, halted only by the drag of the pawls. If the winch is stiff or the pawls fail to click properly, the winch needs at best to be dismantled, cleaned, and lubricated; but the condition could be more serious. Winches almost always contain dissimilar metals, and if they are not properly cared for, corrosion can do serious damage. To fully determine the condition of a winch, you must dismantle it.

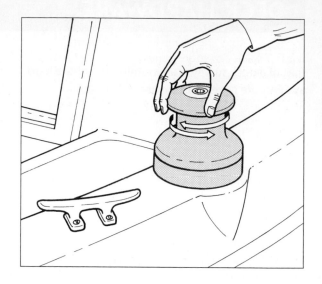

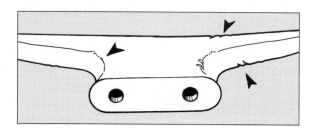

## CLEATS

Run your fingers over all cleats, especially under the horns. Cleats should have no sharp edges and no rough areas, and they should be of an appropriate size for the line they are intended to belay.

## HINGES

Hinges essential to keeping water out of the interior of the boat should be cast or machined from solid bronze or stainless steel and should have oversize pins. Anchor lockers seem especially prone to inadequate hinges (and ridiculous latches if they have one at all). Watch out for cast zinc (Zamak) hardware, which looks strong enough but isn't.

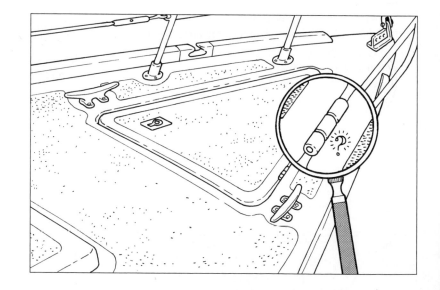

## PULPITS

Both the pulpit and the pushpit should feel strong and rigid. A flimsy pulpit is dangerous. Tubing diameter should be at least 1 inch, and welds should be continuous and well finished.

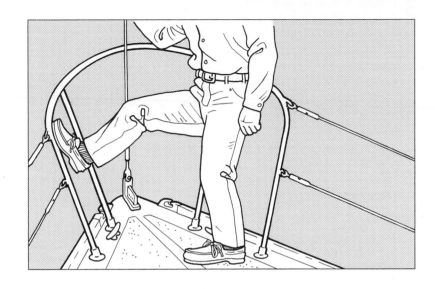

## STANCHIONS AND LIFELINES

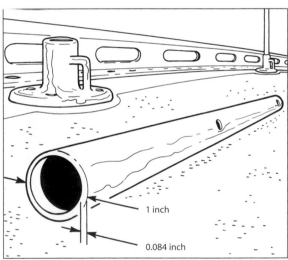

1 inch

0.084 inch

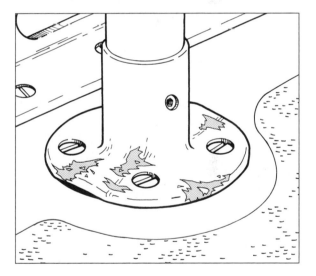

**1** Stanchions made of ⁷/₈-inch, 16-gauge tubing will bend with as little as 130 pounds of pressure, woefully inadequate to stop a flying body (yours). Check stanchions to make sure they are at least 1 inch in diameter and at least 14 gauge—that is, a wall thickness of 0.084 inch.

**2** Proper spacing for stanchions is 6 to 8 feet. In addition to being through-bolted to metal backing plates, the stanchion bases should exhibit no signs of distortion. Peeling plating suggests that the base is zinc, a poor substitute for bronze or stainless steel.

**3** Lifelines tend to fail where the line passes through stanchions and at the end fittings. Examine ends carefully, especially under locknuts. If the fittings are swaged, examine them for cracks with a magnifying glass. Rust appearing through the plastic covering of the cable suggests crevice corrosion, and the safest course is to condemn the wire and replace it.

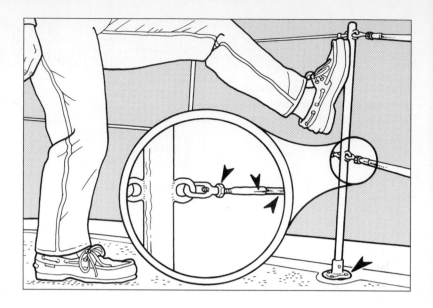

## TRACKS AND TRAVELERS

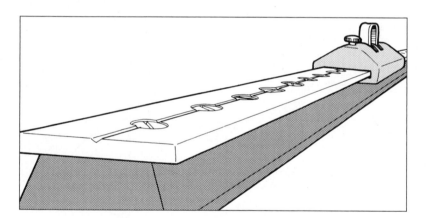

Sight along tracks to observe their contour. Tracks and travelers should be adequately stiff and fastened well enough to remain flat. Track cars should slide easily. Cars on a traveler should move easily even under substantial load.

# CANVAS

Most sailboats have at least a canvas cover for the furled mainsail. Many boats exhibit a wide array of exterior canvas items.

## COVERS

Compare the underside of the canvas to the exposed side; little discernible difference suggests the canvas has a number of years left. Feel the canvas and flex it; acrylic canvas is stiff like brown paper when new, soft like flannel when it is nearing replacement time. Examine all seams for broken or worn stitching.

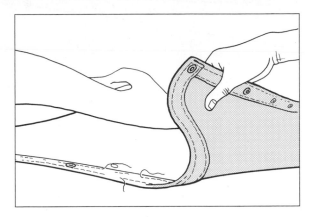

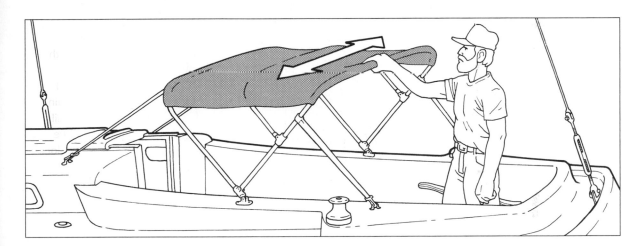

## DODGERS AND BIMINIS

Check the condition of the canvas and stitching as above. Dimple the top with your finger and pour water into it; leakage means the top is near the end of its life. Check for torn or corroded fasteners. Fogged plastic windows will require replacement. Move the frame side to side; some movement is almost unavoidable, but it should be slight for a dodger and not excessive for a Bimini. Because they invariably serve also as a handrail, flexible frames can be dangerous. If the boat will be used outside protected waters, frames should be $7/8$- or 1-inch heavy-wall (14-gauge) steel tubing, and the hinges and mounting hardware should be steel or bronze, not zinc or plastic.

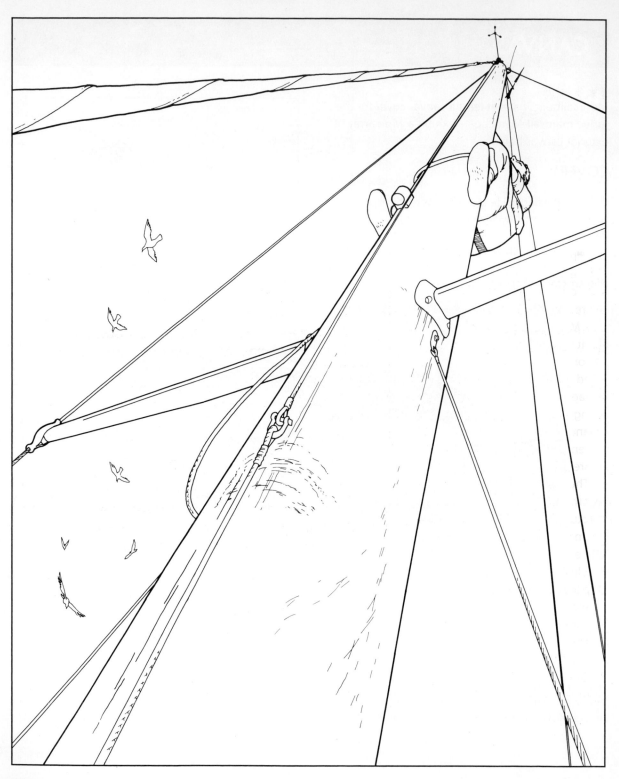

# RIG

The rig is a sailboat's engine. As with any engine, the failure of a single component can leave you dead in the water, but a rigging failure is also likely to drop the mast like an axed pine. Murphy's Law gives you a clue as to which way it will fall relative to your location on the boat; and once the mast ricochets over the side, your vexed boat will try to commit hari-kari by jerking the jagged mast into the side of the hull with each rolling wave. Even if you sail only on Lake Tranquillity and your fine German auxiliary diesel has only two engine hours on it, it is the height of folly to ignore the rig.

The mast and guy wires holding the TV antenna over the roof of your bungalow is essentially a fixed structure, but a sailboat rig is essentially a machine. The mast jerks at the wires and fittings with each tack, each jibe, each passing wave. Hanks slide over wire, lines run over sheaves, and booms lift and drop like a wind-speed indicator. Even when you are motoring along on a calm day, the wires and fittings are dancing to the piston's beat. The tensions result in stretching and distortion, the constant motion in wear and fatigue.

On top of all of this is the issue of exposure, often compounded by the abundant presence of corrosive salts. It is a marvel that sailboat rigs hold up as well as they do. One thing is for certain: destructive forces are at work every day on your rig, and if you aren't on the lookout for them, something will eventually succumb, perhaps with disastrous, even deadly, consequences. Inspecting the rig is not merely advisable; it is an essential responsibility of sailboat ownership.

Much of what you need to inspect is four stories or more overhead, so surveying the rig is much easier when the mast is out of the boat. But the rig should be gone over completely at least every year; so unless you pull the mast that often, plan on an annual trip to the "truck" in a bosun's chair. Pay attention to the safety issues—two halyards, a safety line around the mast, and no snapshackles—and there is no reason that you can't look forward to these ascensions. Take a camera up with you and shoot a few pictures of the masthead; later they will come in handy to show you what shackle or block you need up there without making two trips. Use the rest of the film for some great overhead shots of your boat.

# MAST AND BOOM

In recent years a handful of production boats have been outfitted with laminated carbon fiber spars, not unlike giant and very stiff fishing rods. The unstayed carbon fiber mast may well be the rig of the future, offering strength, light weight, and simplicity, but for now masts and booms are almost invariably extruded aluminum. Surveying a fiberglass sailboat will likely require an evaluation of aluminum spars.

## STRAIGHT

It is desirable to examine spars when they are out of the boat and well supported on several level horses, but this isn't always possible. If the mast is up, release the tension on all the stays and shrouds to allow the mast to take its natural shape. With your eye at the heel of the mast, sight toward the masthead to check for any fore-and-aft or athwartship bend. On horses, roll the mast 180 degrees to separate sag from bend. If you can take the curvature out of a standing mast with hand tension on a shroud, the bend is of no consequence. If the mast exhibits a kink or an S-curve, consult a sparmaker.

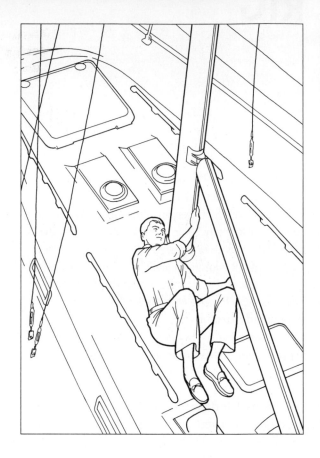

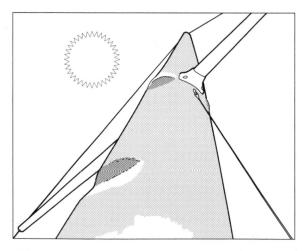

## DENTS AND RIDGES

Spars get much of their strength from the curvature of the tube walls. A sizable dent in a spar is a serious defect and may weaken a spar enough to make it untrustworthy. Booms may show the effects of banging against the rigging during an all-standing jibe. Sight the length of the spar all the way around. Look also for ridges that can occur when an unsupported section of the mast "pumps" unabated for years. If you find dents or ridges, consult a sparmaker. Spars sometimes exhibit slight regular undulations that can occur during manufacture and are of no consequence.

# CRACKS

The usual alloy in aluminum booms and masts is 6061—strong but brittle. The walls of an aluminum spar will crack if overstressed. Examine the mast and boom carefully around every piece of attached hardware, looking for cracks radiating from the fastener holes. Pay special attention to the spreader base area on a mast, and to center-sheeting or hydraulic-vang attachment points on a boom. Also check for splitting at the ends of the spar caused by corrosion swelling of the end caps.

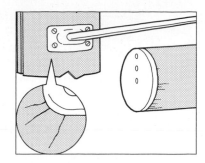

# WELDS

Tapered masts are welded at the top, and the full length of the weld(s) should be examined for cracks with a magnifying glass or a loupe. Examine all other welds on the mast, especially the ends of the welds—where cracks usually start. Welding is common in spar manufacture, but be suspicious of welded repairs since welding destroys the temper of the surrounding aluminum.

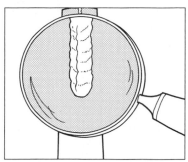

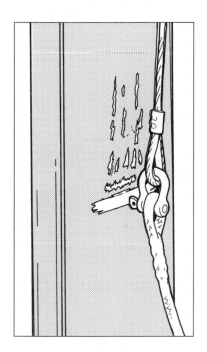

# SURFACE CONDITION

Most aluminum spars are anodized; a few are coated with polyurethane. Either treatment will protect an aluminum spar for decades as long as the coating remains intact. Unfortunately breaches are common, some accidental from chafe, others made purposely when hardware is mounted to the mast. Look for scars in the spots where halyard shackles or eyesplices lie against the mast with the sails both up and down. Tying off external halyards and giving the mast an annual coat of wax goes a long way toward extending the life (and maintaining the appearance) of a mast.

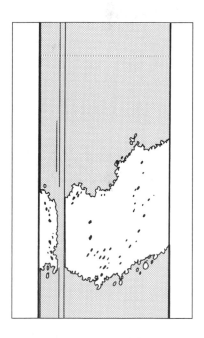

**Oxidation.** For all metal parts on a sailboat, corrosion is the enemy, but on aluminum it is also a friend. The white powdery coating of oxide that forms on the surface of aluminum tends to protect the underlying metal from further corrosion. A surface coating of oxide has little significance regarding the integrity of a spar, but it does tell you that the anodizing is no longer protecting the aluminum. It is time to have the spar reanodized or painted.

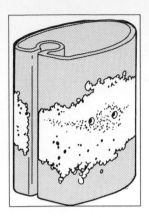

**Corrosion.** Pitting is another matter. If the corrosion has progressed to the point that the surface of the metal is heavily pitted, the strength of the spar has been compromised. You can estimate the extent of the damage by gauging the depth of the pitting and comparing it to the wall thickness of the spar. For example, if the pitting seems to be about $\frac{1}{10}$ of the wall thickness, 10 pits are approximately equivalent to a pit-size hole in the mast. Estimate the number of pits, divide by 10, then multiply that number by the area of a single pit-size hole ($\pi r^2$) and compare the result with the area of a pair of ¼-inch holes (0.10 square inches); a couple of in-line hardware-mounting holes in a mast have little effect on the spar's strength. If your result is much greater, the spar is weakened. Always err in your depth estimates on the side of safety.

## HIDDEN CORROSION

**1** Damaging mast corrosion is most likely to occur at the heel of the mast, especially if it sits in a wet bilge area or if the step lacks an adequate drain. Unfortunately, the corrosion is likely to be on the inside of the mast, one reason the mast must be out of the boat to conduct a thorough survey. If corrosion is breaking through at the heel of a standing mast, damage is almost certain to be extensive and require a new mast or a spliced replacement section at the heel, unless you are willing to shorten the spar.

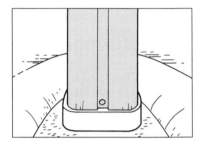

**2** Corrosion is likely at the partners, especially where the boot clamps to the spar. Remove the boot to check. Corrosion may also be hidden by the deck collar and the wedges, but this is less likely if the area under the boot is corrosion free.

**3** Attaching stainless steel fittings or using stainless steel fasteners on an aluminum spar leads to galvanic corrosion. To inspect the mast under fittings attached with threaded fasteners, lubricate the screws with penetrating oil, then remove them with an impact driver to avoid rounding the slot. Rivets have to be drilled out. If the threads in mounting holes are in good shape, clean them with a wire brush (or "chase" them with a tap) and reinstall the fitting. Insulate the fitting from the mast by bedding it in silicone. Coat fastener threads with a locking compound (Loctite) or a corrosion inhibitor (Tef-Gel).

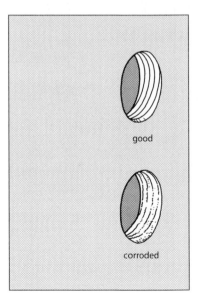

good

corroded

# STEP

The mast step holds the bottom of the mast in position and must take the compression load exerted by the mast when the rigging is tensioned. Mast steps should be troublefree, but there are problems to be on the lookout for.

## DECK STEP

**1** If the deck is dished around the mast step, the support below deck—typically a bulkhead or a beam—is inadequate or perhaps rotten.

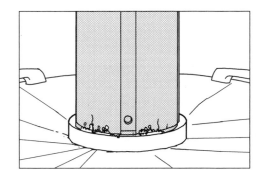

**2** The mast step often sits on a wooden or laminated base to spread the load. Spike a wooden base to check for rot.

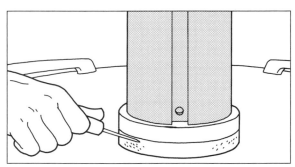

**3** Make sure the step has a good drain that isn't plugged. Water standing inside the mast quickly results in damaging corrosion.

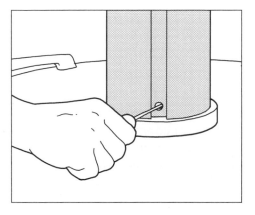

## KEEL STEP

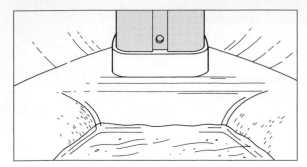

**1** The mast should never be stepped directly on the keel. It should sit on a reinforced floor to transfer the load to the hull and to keep the heel of the mast above any bilge water.

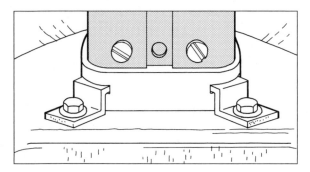

**2** Should the rigging fail, the heel of the mast could cause serious damage and even injury if it comes free of the step. Make sure the mast is bolted to the step and the step is bolted or clamped to the floor.

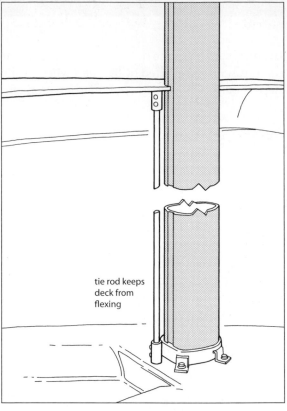

tie rod keeps deck from flexing

**3** Make sure the step has a good drain that isn't plugged. A well-secured bulkhead or a tie rod near the partners is required to keep the deck from moving up the mast.

## PARTNERS

A keel-stepped mast should have a weather boot clamped tightly around the mast and the deck flange; check below for telltale signs of leakage. Check also that the mast is properly aligned and securely wedged at the partners. A canvas coat over the boot adds years to the boot's useful life.

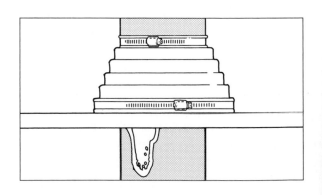

# CAP

The cap fitting at the top of the mast usually provides attachment points for stays, cranes for halyard blocks, and a base for masthead gear like lights and wind indicators. Corrosion is less likely at the cap fitting than at the heel fitting, but if the mast is out of the boat, it is a good idea to remove the cap fitting in order to check the inside of the mast. In any case, go over the cap fitting carefully, looking for cracks at welds and bends and for wear where the rigging is attached.

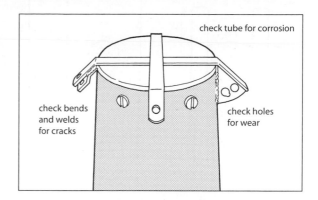

check tube for corrosion

check bends and welds for cracks

check holes for wear

## SHEAVES, BLOCKS, AND HALYARDS

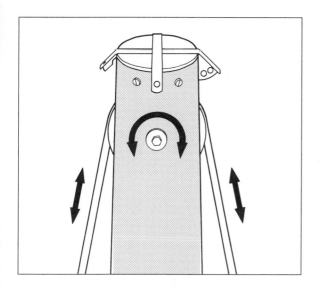

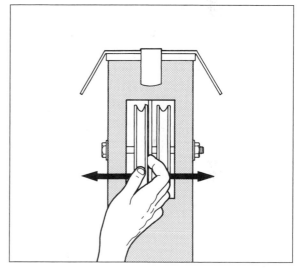

**1** Also at the masthead are the sheaves for the main and jib halyards. Bearings aren't necessary for the low-speed rotation of sheaves, but make sure the sheaves rotate with the movement of the halyards. If the sheaves jam under load, it results in wear of both the halyard and the sheave, and makes sail hoisting and dousing more difficult. Greasing the axle bolt may be all that is required to correct this situation.

**2** Check for side-to-side play of the sheaves. If the halyard can jump the sheave and jam, someday it will, and at the worst possible time. Shimming the side plates should solve this problem.

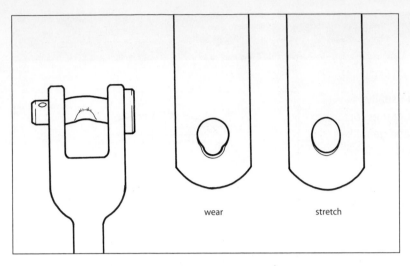

wear          stretch

**3** Check all clevis pins that attach rigging or halyard blocks to the cap fitting. Pins should be straight and unworn. Check also the holes in the cap fitting for elongation. Some elongation as a result of wear is tolerable, but if an aluminum fitting shows any sign of having been stretched, failure is imminent.

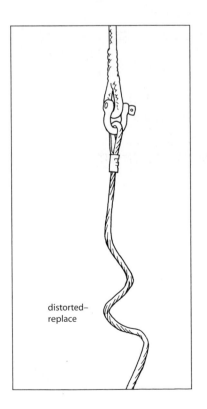

distorted–
replace

**4** Now is a good time to check halyards. Wire halyards that exhibit any broken strands or are kinked or curled must be replaced. Rope halyards should not show wear or have the sisal-like stiffness that signals the weakening effect of sun damage. Check also splices and shackle attachments.

## TANGS

Cap shroud tangs are sometimes a feature of the cap fitting, but more often they are attached below the cap with a bolt that passes through both tangs and the mast. Lower shroud tangs may be similarly attached or part of the spreader socket. Look for mast corrosion under the tang, and distorted holes or mounting bolts. The safest course is to pull tang bolts to check for corrosion. Tangs often develop cracks where they are bent, so examine all bends—on both sides of the tang—with great care, at least with the aid of a magnifying glass and preferably with a dye penetrant, crack-detection process (Spot Check).

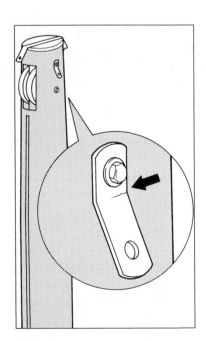

## MASTHEAD GEAR

While you are at the top of the mast, check to see that all masthead lights work. Check antenna and wind instrument mountings as well as the condition of the equipment. Be certain the radio is not on. Examine all exposed wiring and make sure it is protected with grommets in all entry holes. On the way down, check the steaming and/or the deck (spreader) lights.

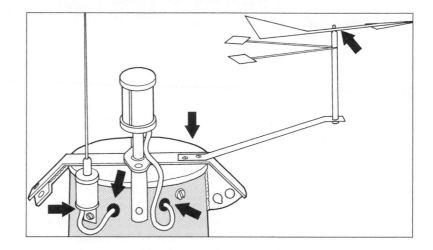

## ASCENDING SAFELY

GOING TO THE TOP of the mast need not be scary or uncomfortable. Every boat should be equipped with a sturdy bosun's chair with around-the-back and between-the-legs straps. First check the halyard carefully, paying special attention to splices and shackle attachments. Using snapshackles is an inherently danger-ous way to attach yourself to the halyard, but if your halyards are fitted with snapshackles, wire the shackle where it cannot be opened. In addition, attach a line to the halyard above the shackle with a rolling hitch and tie it to the lift ring on the chair. Now rig a safety line with a loose rolling hitch around the mast and attach it to the chair, or for greater safety, to a sailing (chest) harness. You will slide the safety line up the mast as you go, and should the halyard drop you, the safety line hitch will tighten and jam against the mast, preventing a fall. Attach a second safety line to allow you to secure yourself above the spreaders before releasing the line below the spreaders. Tying this extra line off to a shackle at the masthead will give you complete confidence in your security while you conduct your inspection.

Reel winches are dangerous for hoisting someone up the mast because the line is never cleated, only held by a friction brake. If you have the help available, going up on dual halyards is the safest method, but you will be momentarily unprotected when you have to unshackle one of the halyards to pass it around a spreader; so use a safety line around the mast even if you are attached to two halyards.

Take up an additional piece of line to serve as a rope step that will allow you to stand and get your eyes above the masthead.

# SPREADERS

Spreaders are especially prone to a number of problems. Spend adequate time examining the spreaders to assure yourself of their soundness.

## CONDITION

Spreaders may be wood, even on an aluminum mast. Wooden spreaders should be finished bright on their underside, so that problems with the wood will be immediately visible, but their top surface should be painted, to better resist exposure. Examine wooden spreaders carefully for checking or splitting. Use a spike or an ice pick to check for rot. Aluminum spreaders are generally superior and less likely to develop problems, but they may corrode where they contact the wire.

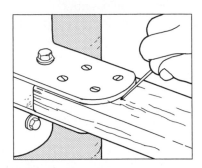

## SOCKETS

**1** Spreader sockets should never be screwed or riveted to an aluminum mast, although far too often that is exactly how they are attached. Pressure on the spreader, such as that applied by a backwinded genoa during a tack, tries to lever the socket off the mast, flexing the mast wall. Move the tip of the spreader and observe the socket; if it moves easily, either the fasteners are loose or the spar wall is cracked. Remove the spreader socket to determine the exact condition.

**2** Unless the spreader sockets are separated by compression tubes or a special compression fitting, tensioning the upper shrouds tends to squeeze the mast. Properly installed sockets are bolted through compression tubes or a fitting that allows the socket to sit snug against the mast but prevents the mast wall from being distorted by the shroud tension. Check the pins in articulating sockets for bend or wear.

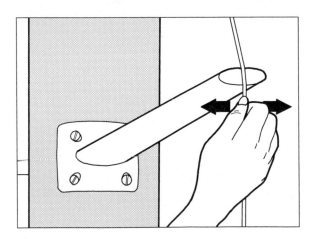

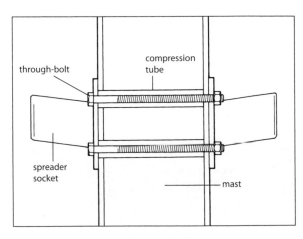

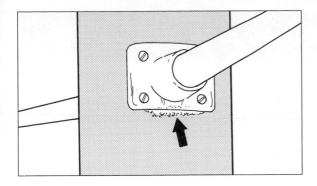

**3** If the sockets are stainless steel rather than cast aluminum, examine the bottom edges of the socket where it lies against the mast. If you find oxidation in the crack between the two parts, the mast is corroding under the socket and you should remove the socket to determine the seriousness of the condition.

## SPREADER TIPS

**1** Wooden spreaders require metal inserts to prevent the wire from splitting the tip. Check to make sure the inserts are there and that the wire has not worn through them.

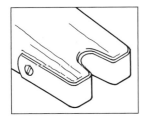

**2** Spreader tips must be secured to the shroud with either clamps or seizing. The tips should be enclosed to protect sails from damage. Rubber boots trimmed to be open on the underside are preferable to rigging tape because they are less likely to encourage corrosion.

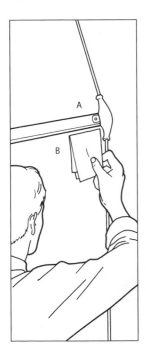

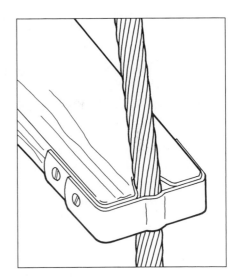

**3** The angle the spreader makes with the wire must be the same above and below the spreader; otherwise the out-of-column compression may cause the spreader to collapse with catastrophic consequences. Take a protractor up the mast with you, or simply fold a sheet of paper to the top angle, then turn it over and check under the spreader.

# GOOSENECKS, SHEETS, AND VANGS

The attachment of the mast to the boom, if it is robust, is generally troublefree except for fastener corrosion. Check for secure attachment. Also examine the fitting for cracks. Roller-furling goosenecks are more complicated and should be tested to see if they operate properly.

Examine bails for wear and for loose or inadequate attachment. Look for signs of corrosion around stainless steel bails. Hydraulic vangs are capable of applying damaging stresses; check around their mount plates carefully.

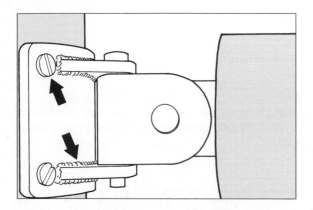

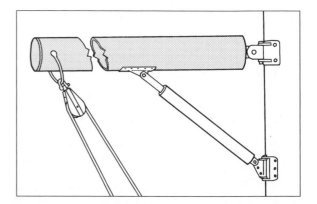

# STAYS AND SHROUDS

Like the battery in your car or the spark plugs in an outboard, stays and shrouds need to be replaced periodically. How long the wire will last depends on how and where the boat is used, but except in extreme conditions, stainless steel rigging should give at least 5 years of service and may well last 15 years or longer.

## WIRE

**1** Typically a matter of design rather than condition, the size of stays and shrouds should nevertheless be checked. As a rule of thumb, the combined strength of the shrouds on one side should be at least 1.5 times the boat's displacement. Stays can be the same size as the shrouds but are often one size larger for added safety and to resist the wear from hanks.

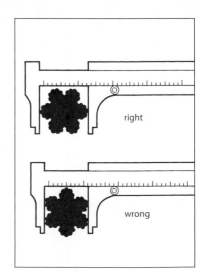

right

wrong

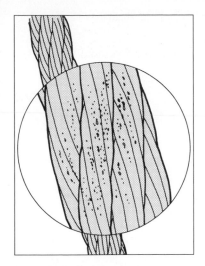

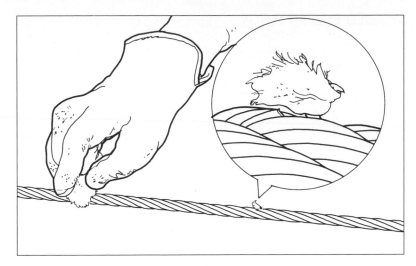

**2** Some uniform discoloration is common with stainless steel rigging, but rigging that is heavily rusted, discolored in some areas but not others, or pitted even mildly should not be trusted.

**3** The classic sign that rigging wire should be condemned is broken strands. Wiping the wire with a cotton ball will flag broken strands, appropriately known as meathooks. A single broken strand, because it is a reliable indicator of the condition of the other strands, is sufficient to condemn a length of wire.

## ROD

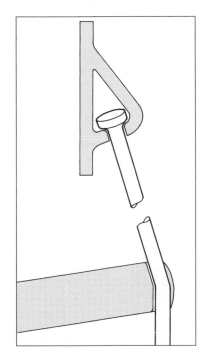

**1** Rod rigging is stronger for its size and stays tuned better, but it gives no warning before it fails. If the failure is not at the formed ends, it is almost always at the point where the rod bends over a spreader. Check both of these areas carefully for cracks.

**2** Discontinuous rod rigging eliminates bend in the rod. Failure is rare, but check the formed ends for cracks or signs of uneven loading.

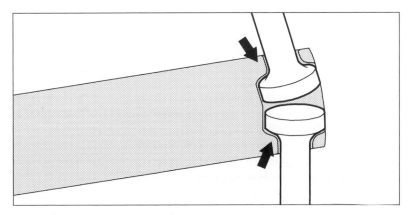

# SWAGED END FITTINGS

Stays and shrouds can be attached by splicing or clamping their ends into eyes, but special end fittings are far more common.

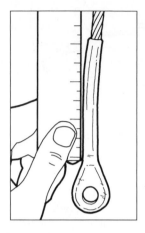 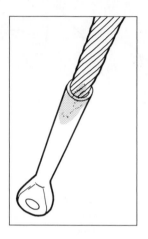 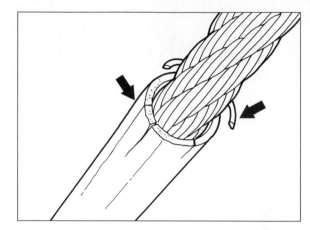

**1** Lay a straightedge alongside the tubular part of swaged fittings. If it is curved—banana shaped— the swage is defective and should be condemned.

**2** Water running down the wire into the interior of the swage leads to corrosion damage. A bloom of rust around the top of lower swaged fittings (upper fittings generally don't have this problem) suggests that the swage has already lost some strength and may soon be untrustworthy.

**3** Swages are rolled onto the wire and depend upon compression for strength. Even a microscopic crack, like unbuttoning a sleeve, will release a swage's grip. Failure of a swage at the deck end of a stay or shroud is by far the most common rigging failure. Examine every swage and condemn any that have cracks. A dye crack detector gives more reliable results.

# MECHANICAL END FITTINGS

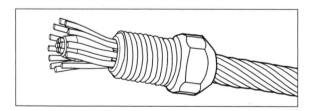 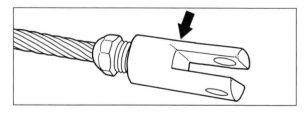

**1** Properly installed mechanical fittings—Sta-Lok and Norseman—are troublefree and can be reused over and over, with replacement of only the internal cone required. If you need assurance that the fitting has been properly installed, open it: the wires should be evenly spaced and close neatly over the cone.

**2** If any fork fittings are installed (eye fittings are almost always preferable), check the base of the jaws carefully. Uneven loading tends to place all the stress on one side of the fitting, leading to failure.

# TURNBUCKLES

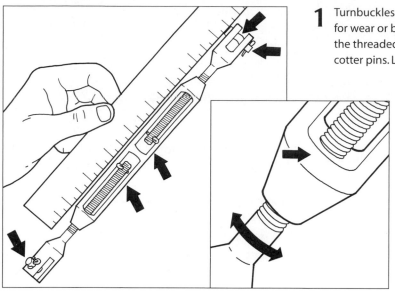

**1** Turnbuckles should be straight. Check the clevis pins for wear or bending. Make sure both the pins and the threaded studs are secured with split rings or cotter pins. Locking nuts on the studs are unreliable.

**2** Stainless steel turnbuckles tend to gall, effectively welding the threaded studs to the body. Check turnbuckles for ease of operation; well-maintained turnbuckles spin easily from fully extended to fully contracted when not under load, but there shouldn't be excessive play in any of the components.

# TOGGLES

There must be a toggle at every deck fitting and at both ends of any stay that carries sail. There is no disadvantage to having toggles at the upper end of all stays and shrouds.

**1** Toggles should be sized properly for the attached turnbuckle. Check for wear, cracks, and bent clevis pins. Pinholes in the surface of a cast bronze toggle are sure signs of "blow holes" in the casting, and the toggle should not be trusted.

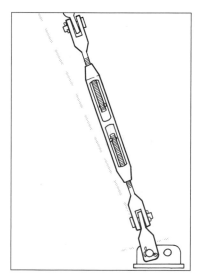

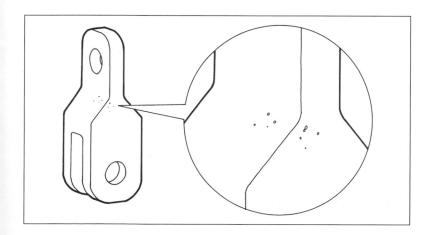

**2** Look for inadequate fork depth, especially at the stem fitting. If the toggle "bottoms out" on the fitting, the pull on the turnbuckle is unfair and will lead to damage or failure.

## TENSION

Excessive rigging tension tends to distort the shape of the boat, sometimes doing permanent damage. Loose stays and shrouds are easier on the boat but can be hard on the rigging in any kind of seaway. Stays and shrouds should be snug but not violin-string tight.

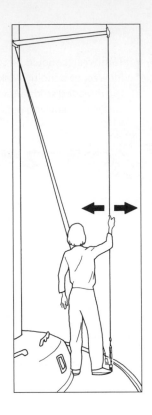

## BACKSTAY ADJUSTERS

Check manual backstay adjusters as you would any other turnbuckle. Check hydraulic adjusters by pumping them to a predetermined tension and then monitoring the gauge for bleed off. Check all fittings for leakage and examine hoses for cracks that signal replacement is required. Make sure the pressure can be released, preferably in a controlled manner that maintains adequate tension on the stay.

## CHAINPLATES

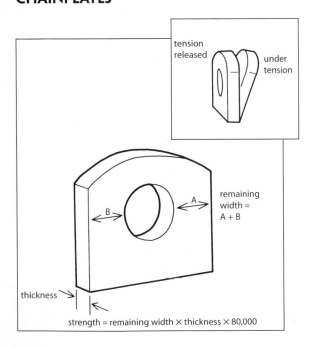

tension released

under tension

remaining width = A + B

thickness

strength = remaining width × thickness × 80,000

**1** Alignment is critical. Relieve the tension on each chainplate and see if it moves out of alignment. Misalignment subjects the chainplate to flexing, and it puts uneven stresses on the pins and jaws of the attached toggle and turnbuckle.

**2** Chainplates should be *at least* as strong as the shrouds they are attached to. Because the load can sometimes be concentrated on one side of the pinhole, it's best if chainplates are twice as strong as the shrouds. To calculate the strength of a chainplate, multiply its thickness by the remaining width (the total width minus the hole diameter), and then multiply that by the per-square-inch tensile strength of the chainplate material—about 80,000 pounds for common stainless steel. Compare your calculation to the strength of the wire (see table on page 63). Watch out for chainplates that have been drilled out for heavier rigging: this can actually weaken them.

**3** Examine chainplates for cracks, especially in bends and around the pinhole. Misalignment causes the strap to flex every time a tack or movement of the mast releases tension on the attached shroud or stay. Motoring can also set up resonant vibrations in the rigging that flex the chainplate hundreds of thousands of times, causing the metal to fatigue. Mast tangs are subject to the same problem.

**4** Water collects around chainplates just below deck level, trapped by the caulking that prevents intrusion into the cabin below. Standing in a collar of water is highly damaging to stainless steel, often leading to crevice corrosion and ultimately to chainplate failure. The only way to inspect a chainplate thoroughly is to remove it and have it X-rayed, or at least do a dye test on it. Any cracks, pits, or other flaws should condemn a chainplate.

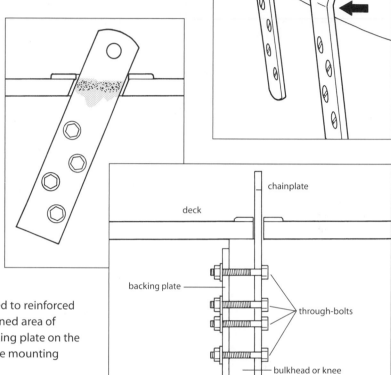

**5** Chainplates should be through-bolted to reinforced bulkheads or knees or to a strengthened area of the hull, and they should have a backing plate on the opposite side. Check the bolts and the mounting holes for wear or distortion.

## BREAKING STRENGTH OF 1 X 19 STAINLESS STEEL (302/304) WIRE ROPE

| Diameter (inches) | Strength (pounds) | Diameter (inches) | Strength (pounds) |
|---|---|---|---|
| 1/16 | 500 | 1/4 | 8,200 |
| 3/32 | 1,200 | 9/32 | 10,300 |
| 1/8 | 2,100 | 5/16 | 12,500 |
| 5/32 | 3,300 | 3/8 | 17,500 |
| 3/16 | 4,700 | 7/16 | 22,500 |
| 7/32 | 6,300 | 1/2 | 30,000 |

—Courtesy of *Rigger's Apprentice.*

**1** Roller-furling design varies with manufacturer, but the requirement to roll the sail under tension is common to all types. Crank extra pressure on the backstay with the backstay adjuster or by tightening the turnbuckle, then open and furl the headsail. It should be quite easy if the sail is luffing; otherwise the furler requires servicing.

**2** Drop the sail to check the luff groove. Sight up the bare extrusion for twists or other defects. Examine the swivel, the halyard, the drum, and the furling line. Rehoist and tension the sail.

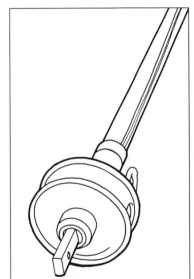

# SAILS

A professional surveyor generally gives sails only the most cursory inspection, often simply listing the inventory and assigning each sail a one- or two-word description of condition—"nearly new," "serviceable," etc. For the purchase of a racer, the only sure way to assess sails—a big portion of the boat's value—is to take a knowledgeable sailmaker aboard and fly each sail in the inventory. For less exacting requirements, you can get a good idea of the quality and condition of the sails aboard by examining them.

**1** Crisp sailcloth suggests that a sail is new or has seen very little use. Old or sunburned sails are soft. Stand on the shady side of a hoisted sail and if it shows pinholes in the panels (not needle holes), it is in its twilight years.

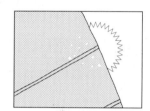

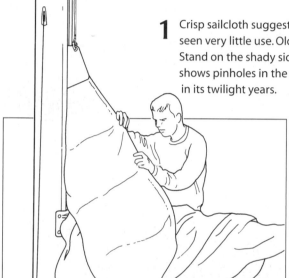

**2** Examine the sail for obvious defects—rips, patches, abrasions, broken stitching, torn cringles. This is easiest if you can spread the sail on a lawn or floor, but you can also inspect a sail by hoisting it incrementally. Examine one side as the sail goes up, the other as you lower it.

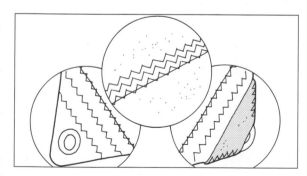

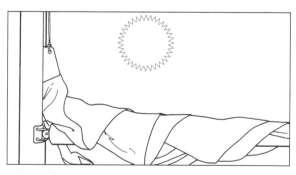

**3** It isn't possible to determine how a sail sets without flying it, but triple stitching at panel seams, heavy corner patches, and hand-finished leather chafe protection suggest quality construction.

**4** If possible, determine where and how the sail has been stowed. Any part of a sail that has been constantly exposed to the sun for a season or two is damaged, even if the rest of the sail is perfect.

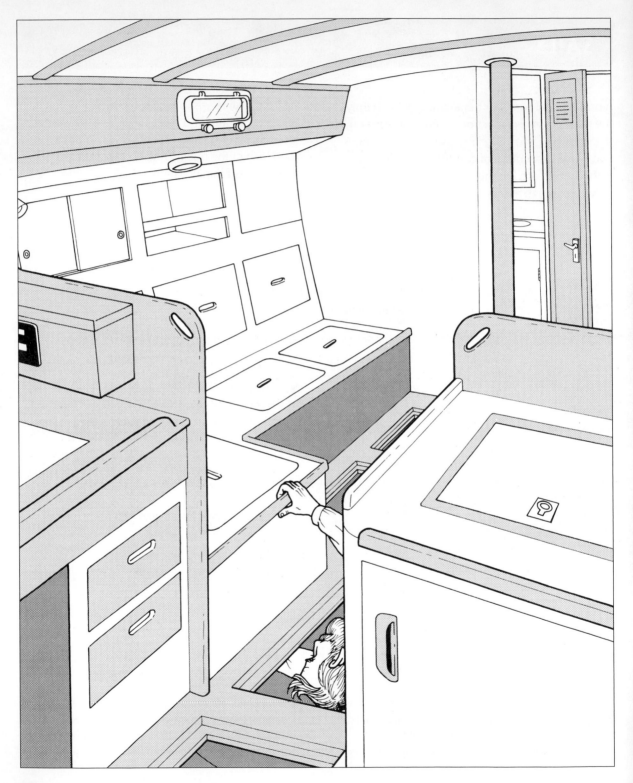

# INTERIOR

Surveying the outside of a boat requires an occasional trip below. You have already been below to check the attachment of the keel, the hull-to-deck joint, and the security of the chainplates. But now we are going to concentrate on the boat's interior components.

The interior of a boat is a trap. Manufacturers discovered long ago that attractive interiors sell boats. If you don't believe it, go to a boat show and compare the amount of time shoppers spend below to the time they spend on deck. Nice woodwork and plush upholstery are essential to getting signatures on the dotted line.

There is nothing wrong with having a great-looking interior—but never use interior decor to judge a boat. Far too many manufacturers building to a budget have scrimped elsewhere to put money into their boats' interiors. This strategy is often successful financially, but intellectually—and perhaps morally—it is bankrupt. Coordinated colors and rubbed varnish don't account for much when the wind pipes up and the seas start to crest.

Don't misunderstand; a cozy, woody interior is a definite plus over a boat with the interior charm of a refrigerator, but you should not be overly influenced by a boat's below-deck look. Treat a fab interior as a bonus or as a tie-breaker, but not as a major selection criterion.

What's behind the wood and fabric is what you're most interested in. Is the deck hardware through-bolted with generous backing plates? Are all through-hull fittings accessible? Are electrical wires secure or are they free to chafe dangerously against raw glass as the boat pitches and rolls? A couple of sheets of veneered plywood can hide a plethora of flaws and omissions. Make sure both the intent and the function of the interior design is nothing more sinister than to give the boat added appeal.

Cabinets and furniture can also seriously complicate some emergencies. Imagine sailing into submerged debris; if the hull was holed below the waterline, could you get to the damaged area to stem the flow from inside?

Look at the cabin of a boat critically. Fight the tendency to form an opinion based on a pleasing decor. Interior varnish and velvet have almost exactly the same significance as a nice shade of red engine paint; they don't give a reliable indication of anything.

# BULKHEAD ATTACHMENT

Rarely are bulkheads installed solely to divide up the living space. They are an integral component of the boat's design, providing critical and essential strengthening, but they must be well attached to do the job.

**1** Bulkheads attach to the hull with laminated strips of fiberglass tape—called tabbing. Check to make sure they are tabbed continuously to both the hull and the deck. Tabbing on only one side of the bulkhead or a single layer of tape are typical deficiencies to look for.

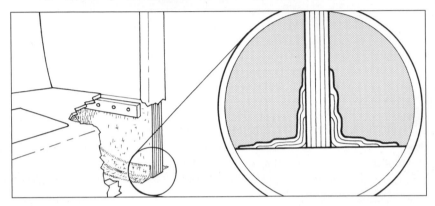

**2** Tabbing rarely comes loose from the hull but often releases from the bulkhead. Use a thin, flexible knife or a feeler gauge to check. If the blade slips between the tabbing and the bulkhead, the bulkhead is adrift. If all the tabbing has released, it will need to be ground away and replaced. Use epoxy resin rather than polyester. For less extensive tabbing failure, you can inject the space with polyurethane adhesive (5200) and reattach the tab with staggered screws. Make sure rigging tension hasn't lifted the bulkhead.

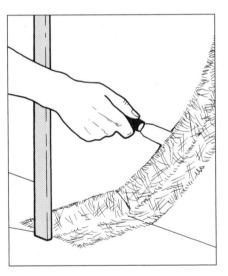

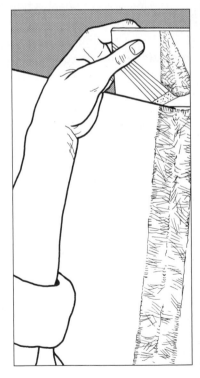

**3** Look at whether the bulkhead sits hard against the hull. To avoid introducing hardspots, bulkheads should sit on foam spacers contoured to also provide a fillet for the tabbing. This is widely acknowledged as the "right" way to install bulkheads, but only the most conscientious builders take the trouble.

# STRINGERS AND FLOORS

Wide expanses of fiberglass are often stiffened by the fore-and-aft edges of built-in furniture, but where furniture is absent, stringers are glassed to the hull. They are sometimes disguised by the construction of a shelf above them. Floors strengthen the hull in the bilge area, supporting the cabin sole and often carrying the stresses from the keel.

**1** Make sure stringers are firmly attached to the hull along their entire length.

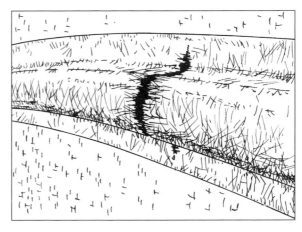

**2** Check the surface of the stringer. Any cracks or tears render the stringer ineffectual. The damage must be repaired and the stringer reinforced.

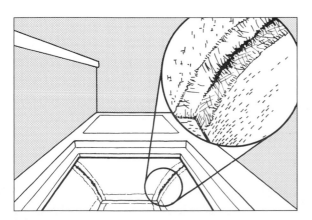

**3** Examine floors for cracks. A hard grounding sometimes breaks floors or tears them from the hull. A tear suggests the repair should include additional strengthening.

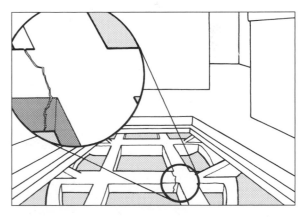

**4** Some boats use a molded interior waffle grid to strengthen the hull and distribute keel and rigging loads. Check every inch of the grid for cracks, and make sure it is securely bonded to the hull.

Fiberglass hull liners have replaced plywood furniture in many production boats. Liners vary from strong and well-engineered structural components to flimsy inserts with purely cosmetic value. In this latter case, the absence of interior reinforcement is likely to allow the hull to flex and distort.

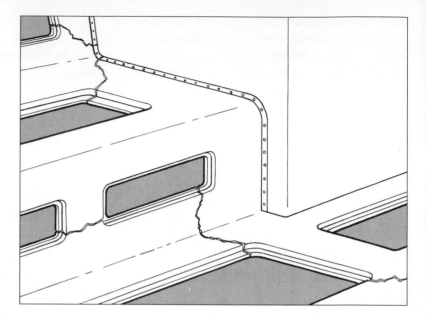

**1** Cracks in the pan suggest inadequate pan strength and hull distortion. In the long term, this can be dangerous.

**2** Poorly designed liners can block access to the hull, a potentially serious flaw in an emergency. Check the liner for hull access.

# DISTORTION

Occasionally an interior bulkhead or beam will prove to be inadequate. Stresses on the hull and deck—typically imposed by rigging tension—bow or buckle the reinforcing member.

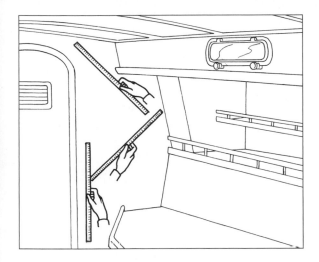

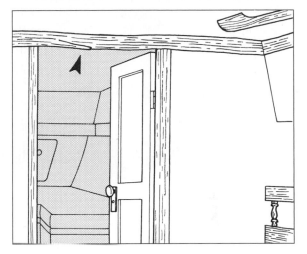

**1** Lay a straightedge in a variety of orientations against one side of every interior bulkhead. Any significant bowing is a serious defect.

**2** Examine support beams for sagging or cracks. Beams with a bit of upward arc are stronger than straight beams.

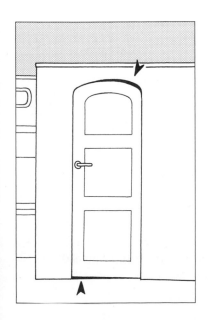

**3** Look at how cabin and cabinet doors fit. If they no longer fit their frames or openings, the interior has changed shape. A head door that drags or jams, for example, typically indicates movement of one of the bulkheads on either side of the opening, probably the one under the mast.

Interior fittings and equipment can be damaged by water—not to mention the discomfort a soggy bunk can cause. The cabin should be virtually watertight.

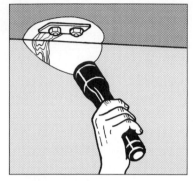

**1** With a strong light, examine bulkheads and the interior of the hull for runnels—water tracks outlined with dust, rust, or salt. The source of such leaks is usually obvious, and the offending gasket or mounting bolt will need to be renewed or rebedded.

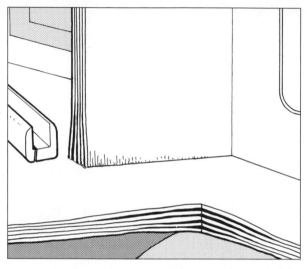

**2** Plywood members and furniture will show signs of delamination if they remain wet. Look especially close at plywood soles and the lower portion of bulkheads.

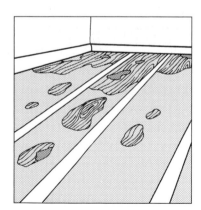

**3** Black stains under varnish or bubbles under paint (or varnish) finishes are sure signs of water damage.

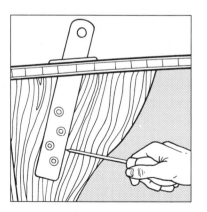

**4** Use a sharpened spike or an ice pick to check interior wood for rot. Spike knees and bulkheads around chainplate attachments; beams and compression posts; sole panels and wooden floors.

# TANKAGE

Replacing a leaking tank can be inordinately expensive because the boat is often built around the tank. Inspect all tanks for condition and security. In a prepurchase survey, you may also want to know the capacity; a close estimate can be made by measuring the tank. To get the capacity in gallons, divide the volume of the tank in cubic inches by 231.

**1** Examine all tanks for construction material. Diesel fuel dissolves zinc, so diesel tanks should not be copper or galvanized. Integral fuel tanks are also a bad idea because fiberglass is not completely impermeable. Fiberglass tanks almost always give water an off taste. Aluminum tanks—all too common in production boats—quickly corrode. Monel is an excellent (but expensive) tank material; stainless steel is less desirable because it is subject to corrosion. Polyethylene provides the best value and fewest problems of any material for all tank applications.

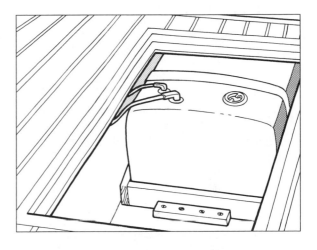

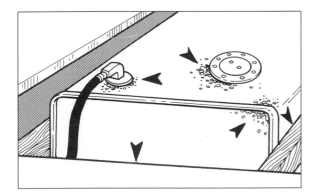

**2** Look for corrosion in steel and aluminum tanks; check the bottom inside the tank and check outside where the tank bears against supports or other parts of the boat. Visually inspect for leakage; if possible, fill the tank and check it again after several days undisturbed.

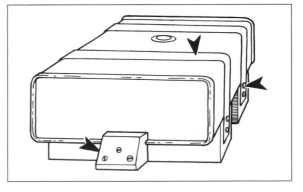

**3** All tanks must be securely mounted, unable to move even if the boat is inverted. Give chocks and straps a thorough inspection. Look for any signs of past movement. Bearing surfaces should be impermeable to discourage moisture retention.

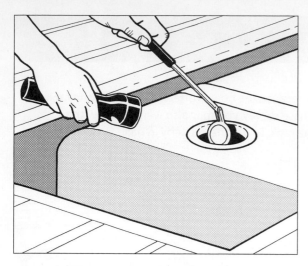

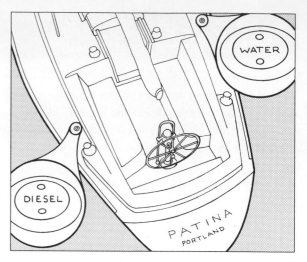

**4** Tanks larger than about 5 gallons should have internal baffles to prevent the liquid from surging inside the tank. Outside weld marks are not a sure sign of baffling; view the interior of the tank through the inspection port with a light and a mirror.

**5** Water and fuel fills should not be near each other, and each should be clearly labeled. Fuel vent fittings should be located as high as possible to prevent water intrusion. Both fill and vent lines (and fuel lines, as well) should be labeled "USCG A1" or "B1."

# HEAD

Discharge laws vary from place to place, but a holding tank and a securable Y-valve to allow direct discharge offshore will meet most state and local codes.

**1** Holding tanks must be vented to the outside to allow the escape of explosive methane.

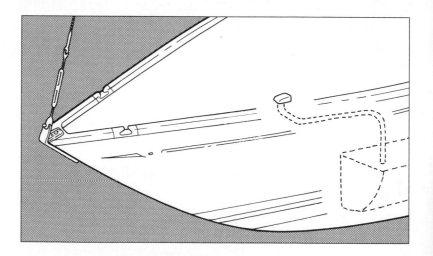

**2** The discharge line from the head must be looped well above the waterline to prevent back-siphoning. If an antisiphon valve is installed in the loop, check its operation by blowing through a piece of hose fitted over the nipple. (To minimize odor from an antisiphon valve, vent it overboard.)

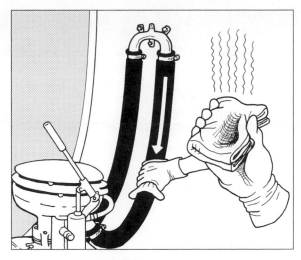

**3** Wipe the outside surface of the discharge line with a damp cloth, then smell the cloth. If it has picked up an odor, the hose is the wrong type for this application.

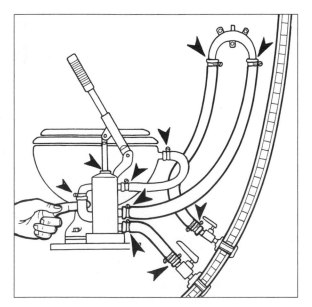

**4** Check the head and all hose connections for fresh signs of leakage.

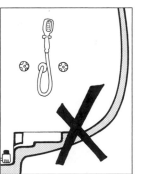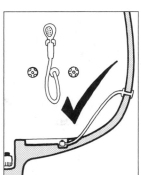

**5** If the boat has a shower, check the drain pan. It should empty quickly into a dedicated sump; draining the shower into the main bilge is a clog hazard that could endanger the boat. Check the operation of the shower sump pump.

The functionality of a galley is more often a matter of design than condition, but there are some universal requirements.

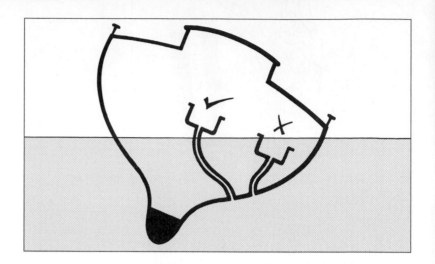

**1** Where is the sink drain? Sinks should be located near the centerline of the boat. Those located near the hull can flood the cabin when the boat heels to that side.

ballast

**2** If the stove will be used underway, it must be gimbaled fore-and-aft, and it must have sufficient ballast to overcome the weight of a full pot sitting on the burner.

PROPANE SWITCH

OFF ⬭ ON    ◯ POWER

TURN OFF WHEN NOT USING

**3** Where propane is the galley fuel, a solenoid shutoff at the tank with a warning light in the galley is essential. The supply line must be continuous from the tank, except for the inclusion of a flexible segment to a gimbaled stove.

**4** Propane tanks must be mounted on deck well clear of any deck openings, or in a vaportight locker with an overboard drain that will not submerge when the boat heels. The bottle(s) should be fitted with a pressure gauge.

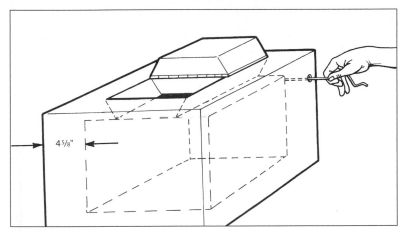

4 5/8"

**5** Factory ice-chest insulation—if there is any at all—is too often a couple of inches of fiberglass batting. To be efficient, a refrigerator or icebox requires a minimum of 4 inches of urethane foam on all sides. Measure the distance between inner and outer walls and subtract about ⅝ inch (for the two skins). Probe to determine the insulation material.

**6** Air-cooled refrigeration should be located where the air flowing across the condenser will be coolest, which means not in the engine room.

# SEACOCKS

The safest number of through-hull fittings is zero. The usual number is at least seven. Always keep in mind that the only thing keeping your boat afloat is the clamps and hoses connected to these fittings.

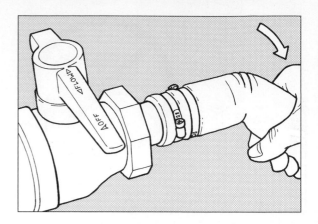

**1** Squeeze or flex all hoses connected to the seacocks. Any that show cracks or hardening require replacement.

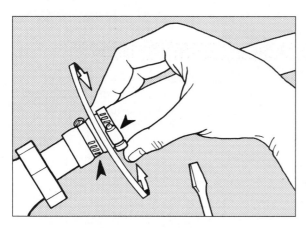

**2** Check every below-the-waterline hose connection for dual clamps. Even all-stainless clamps corrode, usually at their lowest point or beneath the screw housing. Loosen each clamp and rotate it 360 degrees to inspect it, then retighten it.

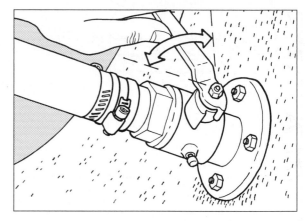

**3** Every through-hull fitting that is (or could be) below the waterline should be equipped with a seacock. Gate valves are inherently unsafe and must not be substituted. Operate each seacock to make sure it is in good working order. Unused seacocks have an annoying tendency to freeze, rendering them worthless, and replacement generally requires a haulout.

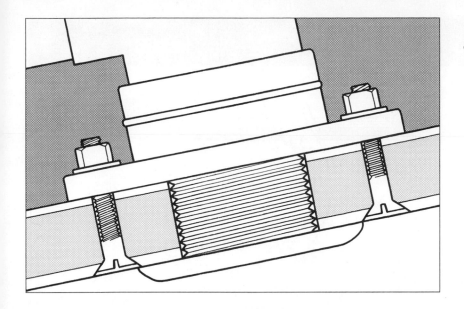

**4** Make sure all seacocks are bolted to the hull, not just threaded onto the through-hull fitting. If the seacock is bronze, the bolts should also be bronze; a pile of corrosion on them will tell you the bolts are steel. Also make sure that the through-hull and the seacock are the same material; never mix bronze and plastic.

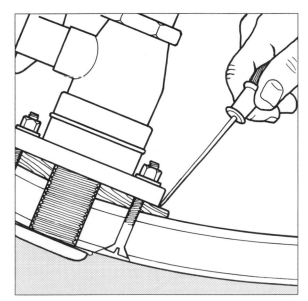

no bolts in flange

gap under flange

**6** Check the seacock for any signs of leakage. Traditional tapered-plug seacocks are particularly prone to leaking, and if the nut has to be so tight to stop the leak that the handle can't be turned, the seacock needs servicing and perhaps replacement.

**5** Seacocks are often installed on backer blocks to accommodate the contour of the hull. If the backer block is wood, spike it to make sure it has not gone spongy.

# BILGE PUMPS

No sailboat bigger than a dinghy should be without at least one bilge pump, and most boats require two or more.

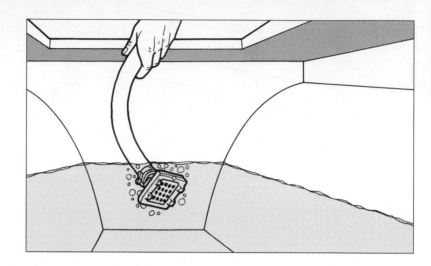

**1** An operable manual bilge is essential equipment even if the boat is equipped with an array of electric pumps. Check the pickup to make sure it is clog protected. Pump the handle to make sure the pump will prime and move water out of the boat efficiently.

**2** Automatic bilge pumps should also have an ON position in case the float switch fails. Run electric pumps to check their operation.

**3** Find where all pumps discharge. Outlets must always remain above water or they will siphon water into the boat, causing the pump to run until it kills the battery; then the boat will fill.

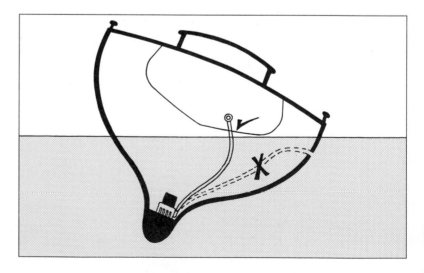

# COMFORT AND SAFETY

While you are in the cabin, consider the design features that have comfort and safety implications. Some can be improved—at your expense. Others you are likely to simply live with.

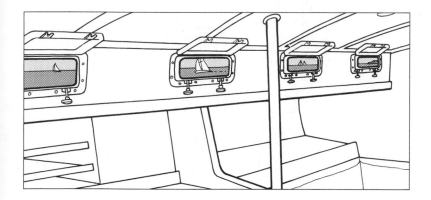

**1** Fixed ports and a single forward hatch make for an uncomfortable boat when the mercury rises. It is unlikely that a boat will have too much ventilation. Check the number of hatches, opening ports, and effective ventilators.

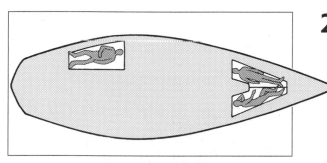

**2** V-berths are great in port—if they are long enough and don't come to a point—but they are worthless at sea. At least one bunk well aft to serve as a sea berth is essential if anyone plans to sleep underway. Check bunks for length (long) and width (not too wide) and location (aft).

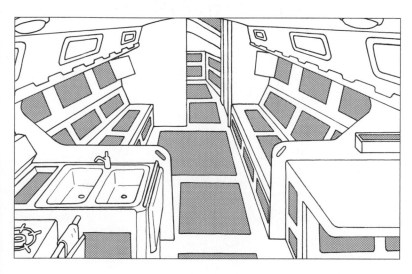

**3** Depending on the intended use of the boat, stowage capacity can be an important factor. A heavier-displacement cruising boat should be able to swallow up a mountain of gear and supplies. Light-displacement boats have less carrying capacity and smaller locker spaces.

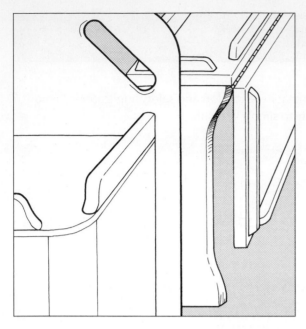

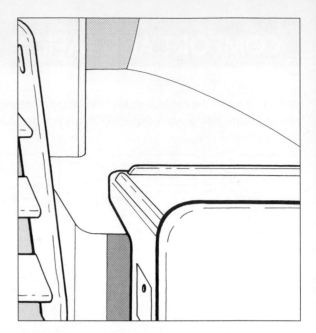

**4** Look at shelves, counters, and tables to see if items will stay put when the boat heels. High fiddle rails can prevent a great deal of irritation and innumerable accidents.

**5** Sharp corners are dangerous in the cabin of a pitching boat. So are wide spaces. Fall against the furniture and other surfaces in the cabin to see if an unexpected fall is likely to cause injury.

**6** Unexpected falls are far less likely if the cabin has ample strong, intelligently spaced handholds. Make sure you can pass from one end of the cabin to the other without releasing your grip.

# DECOR

Now you can admire the varnished trim and the beautiful fabric on the settee cushions. So they're pretty, but what condition are they in?

**1** Check all the upholstery for soiling, wear, tear, and open seams. Pay special attention to zippers: metal zippers are almost certain to be corroded beyond use, and so are plastic zippers if the slide is metal.

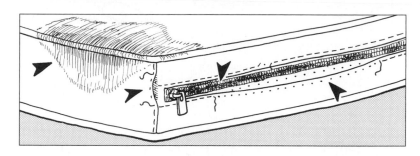

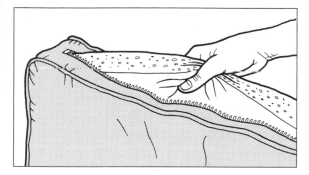

**2** Check the foam. Firm foam is essential for comfort. Old foam tends to crumble and go soft. Quality replacement foam can be expensive.

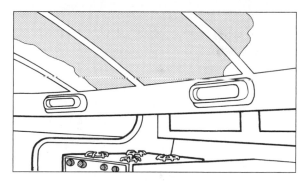

**3** If the headliner is fabric, observe its color and condition. Some vinyls tend to yellow with age, and all can be affected by galley smoke.

**4** Look at the condition of mica on bulkheads, tables, and countertops. Burns and some stains are permanent.

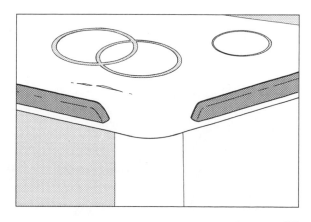

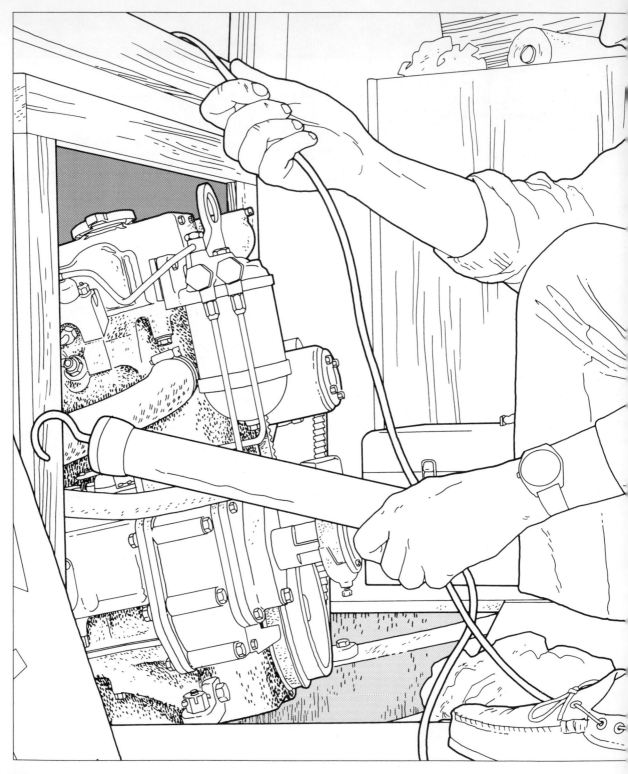

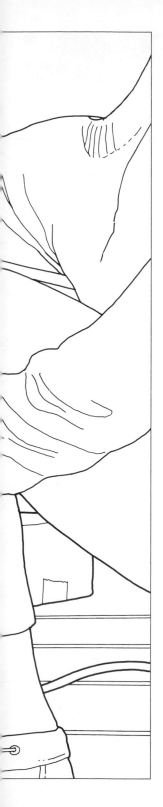

# ENGINE AND STEERING

It is time to remove engine hatches and cockpit-locker panels and examine the other half of the interior, the half occupied by the engine, cables, filters, and steering gear.

A truly comprehensive evaluation of the condition of an inboard engine requires a specialized examination by a qualified marine mechanic. In-depth engine evaluations are generally beyond the capability of even a professional surveyor. But there are key indicators that can give you a reasonably good idea of the condition of a boat's engine.

A lot of obvious engine problems go undetected for a long time because engine spaces are almost always dark. The most important engine-surveying tool is a bright light. A fluorescent drop light is ideal.

In this chapter, our focus is primarily on diesel engines. Gasoline engines have not been installed in production sailboats in the United States for more than 20 years. There are still thousands of older sailboats with gasoline engines, of course; but since a gasoline engine doesn't add value to the boat, there is little need to know more than whether the engine runs and meets stringent safety requirements. When a gasoline engine reaches the end of its useful life, most owners elect to repower with diesel.

Outboard engines are omitted here altogether. It is a simple matter to take an outboard engine in the sizes generally found on a sailboat to a qualified outboard mechanic for testing.

An oil-coated engine and black bilges have always suggested indifferent maintenance, but today they have additional implications. Pumping out oily bilge water can result in a substantial fine. It is now even more important for an engine to be well maintained and for bilges to be kept clean.

If you are surveying your own boat, you already know about the access compromises the manufacturer made in order to minimize the interior space lost to the engine installation. There are boats in which the stuffing box is only accessible once the engine is removed. The time to discover such absurdities is before you buy. Here is a sample of access questions, but in general you should be able to get to every side of the engine.

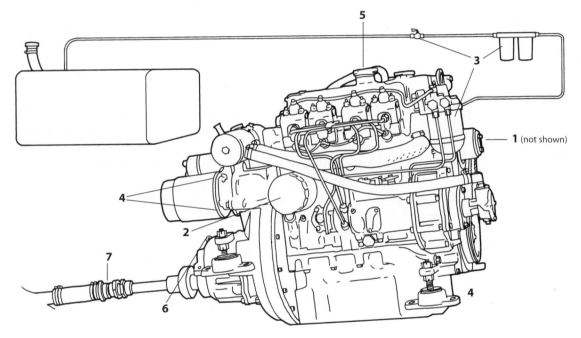

**1** Where is the raw-water pump? Flexible impellers have to be replaced periodically—and it should be a simple job.

**2** Can you get to the oil filter? Can you get a strap wrench around the canister and have room to turn it?

**3** Are the fuel filters likewise accessible, and can you easily reach the fuel-supply shutoff valve?

**4** Can you get a wrench on both starter mounting bolts? What about servicing the alternator?

**5** Is there room above the oil filler to turn up a can of oil?

**6** Can you reach the transmission dipstick?

**7** Can you get two wrenches on the stuffing box? If so, will you be able to apply enough force to release and retighten the locknut?

# VISUAL CLUES

Shine a bright light on the engine and look it over slowly and carefully with a critical eye. Streaks, cracks, stains, and shiny spots all need explanation.

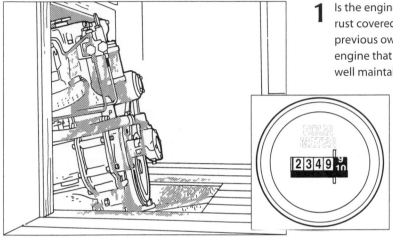

**1** Is the engine clean and nicely painted or dirty and rust covered? This may tell you more about the previous owner than about the engine, but an engine that looks new is more likely to have been well maintained.

How many hours does the engine have? A functioning hour meter is essential for properly scheduling maintenance. A well-maintained auxiliary diesel should easily run 5,000 hours between overhauls. Well-kept maintenance logs are a major plus.

**2** Look for leaks of any kind. Touch your finger to the underside of all hose and fuel connections. Rub across the bottom of the fuel pump and all fuel filters. Check bleed screws on the injector pump. Examine the catch pan under the engine and the bilge for dripping oil.

**3** Squeeze all coolant hoses; if they're hard and brittle, soft and spongy, or cracked, they need replacing. Look for kinks that might restrict flow. Examine both hoses and fuel lines anywhere they might be rubbing; the lively movement of a running diesel can quickly wear through a chafing line.

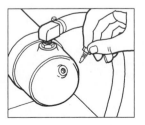

Check the zinc pencil on the heat exchanger. If it is badly corroded or missing, check the exchanger more carefully for evidence of corrosion.

**4** Open the pressure cap on the expansion tank; if it feels oily, dip some of the coolant out into a clear glass and let it settle. Oil in the coolant suggest a blown head gasket (bad) or a cracked water jacket (worse).

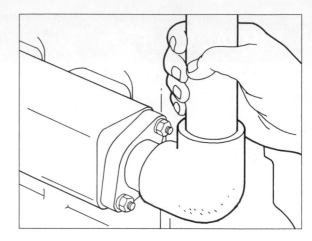

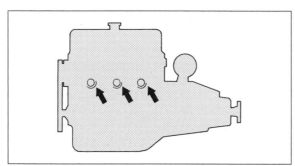

**5** Check the exhaust system from the engine to the transom. Be especially suspicious of copper or stainless steel standpipes and water-jacketed exhausts. Give the section that connects to the manifold a good jerk; hot diesel gases eat at the pipe, eventually loosening or destroying it.

**6** Locate every freeze plug and examine each for signs of rust or leakage.

## GASOLINE ENGINES

GASOLINE IS VERY DANGEROUS in a boat because it is highly volatile and the heavier-than-air fumes can collect in the bilge. If you are inspecting a boat with a gasoline inboard, there are additional things to look for.

1. Does the tank show any signs of corrosion? A leaking tank can be deadly.
2. The potential consequences of a gasoline tank coming adrift are horrific, so make especially sure the tank is securely chocked and strapped.
3. Are all connections to the top of the tank? Bottom fittings are both dangerous and illegal.
4. The fill pipe should be flexible, not rigid, and the vent line must be outboard and equipped with a flame arrestor screen.

5. Are both the tank and the deck fill electrically grounded to the engine to bleed off static electricity?
6. Is the deck fill located where an overflow cannot enter the boat?
7. A functioning fuel shutoff at the tank is mandatory.
8. Look for flexible—not rigid—fuel lines rated for gasoline. Spring clamps should never be used on gasoline lines. Make sure the separator bowl isn't glass.
9. The carburetor must be down-draft and equipped with an approved flame arrestor.
10. Make sure the boat has a functional bilge blower, vented overboard, with the pickup in the lowest dry part of the bilge. An intake vent lower than the carburetor intake is also required.

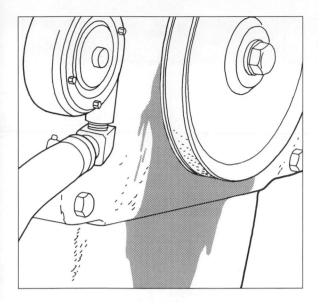

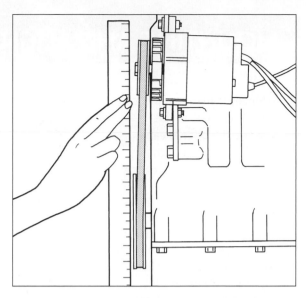

**7** Check both the front and the back of the engine for signs that either oil seal is leaking.

**8** Check the engine and the surrounding bulkheads for telltale black fluff that indicates excessive belt wear. If you find belt fluff, check the alignment of the various pulleys with a straightedge. Misalignment can be a serious problem or one easily solved with spacers. A corrosion-roughened pulley can also be the problem.

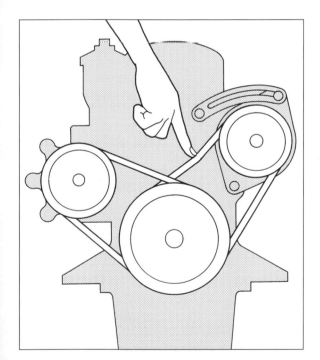

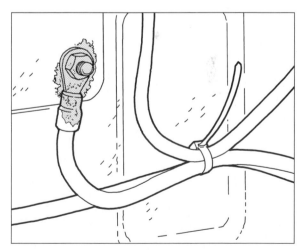

**9** Check belt tensions. With moderate finger pressure, you should be able to depress the longest span about $3/8$ inch.

**10** Examine all wiring connections for corrosion and all wire runs for support.

Occasionally someone reports that the engine fell off the bearers into the bilge. It can't be a pleasant event, but there were almost certainly adequate warning signs.

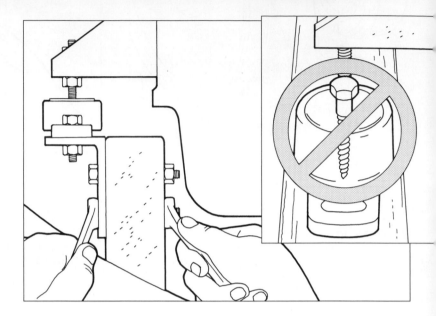

**1** Check the engine mounts. Put a wrench on every nut and bolt that attaches the mounts to both the engine and the bed to make sure they are tight. Engine mounts are too often secured to the bearers with lag screws; where heavy weather is possible, mounts must be through-bolted to the bearers.

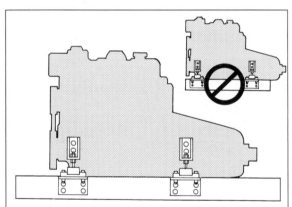

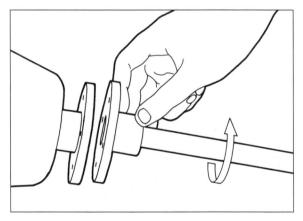

**2** The engine bearers under a diesel need to be robust to take the punishment; they should be substantially longer than the engine. Be particularly suspicious of the bearers in a boat that has been repowered from gasoline to diesel. Check the bearers closely to make sure they are securely attached to the hull. Check wooden bearers for splits, cracks, and rot.

**3** Rotate the propeller shaft to check for alignment. A short shaft with a rigid coupling will not show misalignment unless you remove the coupling bolts and separate the coupling slightly. Misalignment can usually be corrected by turning the adjustment nuts on the engine mounts, but this should only be checked and adjusted with the hull afloat. Flexible couplings are not a substitute for good engine alignment.

# STUFFING BOX

Fiberglass sailboats generally pass the prop shaft to the outside of the hull in the least complicated way—through a tube glassed into the hull and connected to the stuffing box with a length of rubber hose. Flax packing in the stuffing box is compressed against the shaft to seal it.

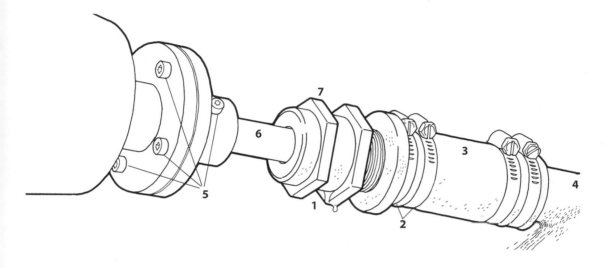

**1** Check the stuffing box for leakage. A slight drip is often recommended to cool the stuffing, but more that six drops per minute is excessive. If tightening doesn't seal the fitting, repacking is needed.

**2** The clamps that are on the hose connecting the stuffing box to the stern tube typically corrode on the bottom. Release and rotate them to check, then retighten. The hose should be double-clamped at both ends.

**3** Check the hose for hardening or splitting. The shaft must be removed—or at the very least extracted from the coupling—to install a replacement.

**4** Check the stern tube carefully for fractures or separation from the hull.

**5** Check all coupling bolts and set screws to make sure they are in place and tight.

**6** Make sure there is adequate space between the coupling and the stuffing box to slide the nut back for repacking.

**7** Come back to the stuffing box and touch it immediately after running the prop for a while. If it is hot, the packing is too compressed and needs to be replaced. Excessive tightening will score the shaft.

# EXHAUST SMOKE

After you have made all your visual inspections, it is time to start the engine. If you're doing a pre-purchase survey, be sure this is the first time the engine has been started today: easy starting of a cold diesel is the best indicator of its overall state.

Position yourself to see the exhaust as the engine starts. A good-running diesel will not smoke at all under load, but it may smoke at start-up and at idle.

**1** White exhaust smoke generally indicates moisture in the cylinders, but it can also suggest low cylinder compression. If the smoke clears up quickly, the cause is probably nothing more than condensation inside the engine. If smoking continues, the engine may have a blown head gasket (or maybe a cracked head). Unfortunately, a normal wet exhaust can also generate white smoke.

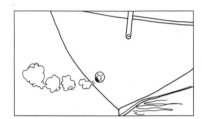

**2** If the exhaust smoke is blue, the engine is burning oil. If the blue smoke continues, suspect the piston rings; the engine needs major work. If the smoke clears up, the valve guides are likely worn and letting oil drain into the cylinder when the engine is stopped. Unless the engine is also hard to start, this condition can probably be ignored until you have other reason to rebuild the head.

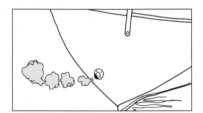

**3** Black smoke is caused by excessive fuel or too little air. If you start the engine using the "cold start" button, black smoke is likely to result, but it should quickly clear. A puff of black smoke is also common when you accelerate, as the engine momentarily overloads. Continuing black smoke usually indicates problems with the injectors or the high-pressure pump; but less serious causes can be motoring into a strong headwind (overloading), a clogged air filter, a restricted exhaust system, or an oversize propeller.

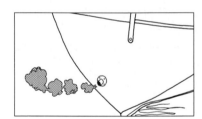

# RUNNING THE ENGINE

One of the best tests of an inboard engine is to run it under load to see exactly how it performs.

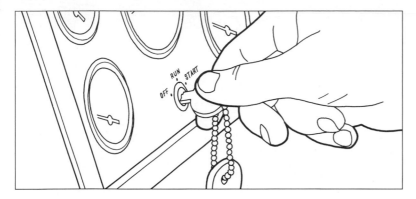

**1** With a fully charged battery, a diesel engine should start easily. Long cranking suggests low compression.

**2** Uneven running at idle speeds is not uncommon, but it should smooth out when the prop is engaged and the engine is put under load. Uneven running under load means one or more cylinders are misfiring. The problem could be something as relatively innocuous as a plugged fuel filter (the misfiring should get worse as you increase the engine speed), or it could be a major—and costly—mechanical problem. It is time for a mechanic.

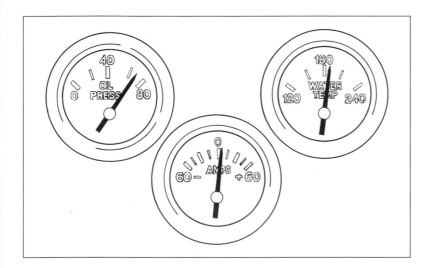

**3** Look at the gauges. After a few minutes under load, oil pressure should be close to what is specified in the owner's manual and the engine should reach optimum operating temperature—about 180 degrees for a freshwater-cooled diesel, 150 for one cooled with raw water. The ammeter should show a substantial charge initially (commonly around 30 amps), a slight tilt to the plus side later.

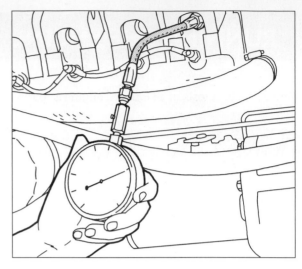

**4** Take another look at the engine and the exhaust system, while the engine is running, to see if they are spewing any liquids or gases. Do the pulleys run true? Diesel engines are notoriously noisy, but do you hear any discordant clanks, any noise that seems extraordinarily loud? Having listened to other diesel engines will prove helpful here.

**5** A compression test is an excellent diagnostic tool. Have a mechanic perform this test, or if you have the equipment, do it yourself. Readings that are consistent between cylinders and close to the engine-maker's specifications (see the owner's manual) suggest that pistons, rings, and valves are all healthy.

## IS THE ENGINE BIG ENOUGH?

THE RULE OF THUMB FOR AN INBOARD auxiliary installation is 3 horsepower per ton of displacement. Of course this also depends on the boat and what you want the engine to do. A narrow, easily driven hull can get away with less power; more will be needed if the boat is beamy and has to shoulder its way through the water. And if you expect to power your way into strong headwinds, you may need 4 or even 5 horsepower per ton.

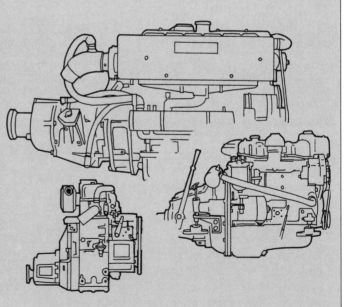

# OIL

After you shut the engine down, pull the dipsticks on both the engine and the transmission. You are interested in more than whether the oil is at the right level.

**1** Bubbles on the engine-oil dipstick indicate water in the sump. The usual source is a failed head gasket, but there are other possibilities. Don't expect the engine oil in a diesel to stay as clear as it does in a gasoline engine.

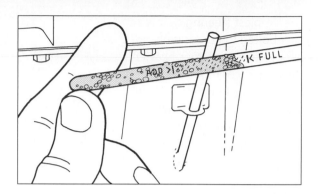

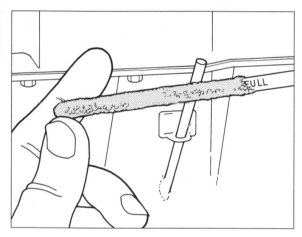

**2** If the engine oil looks like a chocolate milkshake, a lot of water has gotten into the oil. This is more typical with raw-water cooling, and is more damaging to the engine. It usually indicates a crack in the water jacket, often caused by overheating due to a scale buildup. A seal failure on a gear-driven water pump can also let water into the oil.

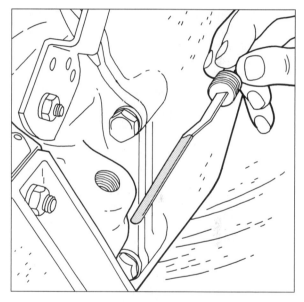

**3** Milky gear-case fluid also indicates saltwater intrusion. In this case, the usual source is a hole in the transmission-oil cooler.

The simplest steering gear is a tiller bolted to the rudderhead, but as boats get larger, heavier steering forces require impractically long tillers. Wheel steering can generate the needed power without sweeping the cockpit.

## RUDDERPOST

**1** Check the rudderstock tube for any signs of separation from the hull.

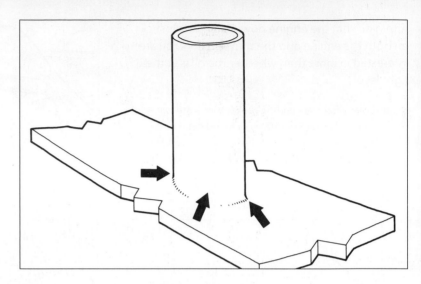

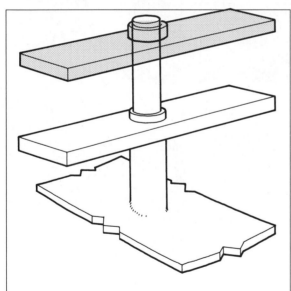

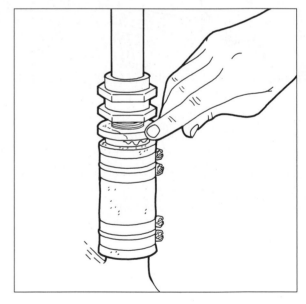

**2** Either the top of the tube or the top of the rudderstock should be rigidly supported. Otherwise the top of the tube is almost certain to move when the rudder is under load.

**3** If the tube ends below the waterline, it will be fitted with a stuffing box. No water should enter the hull around the rudderstock.

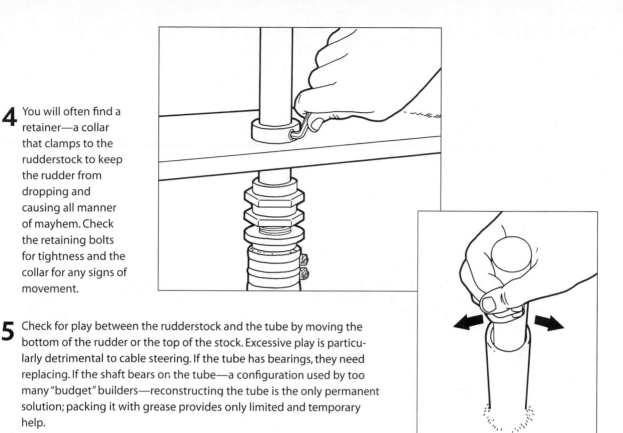

**4** You will often find a retainer—a collar that clamps to the rudderstock to keep the rudder from dropping and causing all manner of mayhem. Check the retaining bolts for tightness and the collar for any signs of movement.

**5** Check for play between the rudderstock and the tube by moving the bottom of the rudder or the top of the stock. Excessive play is particularly detrimental to cable steering. If the tube has bearings, they need replacing. If the shaft bears on the tube—a configuration used by too many "budget" builders—reconstructing the tube is the only permanent solution; packing it with grease provides only limited and temporary help.

## TILLERS

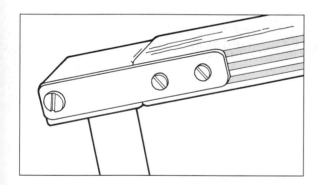

**1** Play in a tiller takes the pleasure out of steering. Check the tiller to make sure the clamp bolt holes are not elongated and the bolts are snug. The tiller should fit tightly to the rudderhead.

**2** Tillers are often laminated from woods that are strong and/or attractive, but not rot resistant. Check the tiller, particularly underneath, for black spots beneath the varnish, and probe its rudderstock end for rot.

# CABLE STEERING

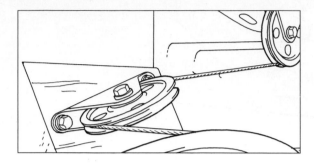

**1** Check the cables for wear and to make sure they aren't loose. Any broken strands mean it is time to replace the cables. With the wheel hard over in both directions, the cables should be just tight enough to give off a musical note when you thump them—but not a high note. Both the sheave bearings and the cables should be well oiled.

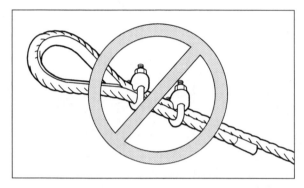

**2** Cable ends should have mechanical fittings (Norseman) or thimbles retained by two compression sleeves (Nicopress); knots or rigging clamps are not acceptable.

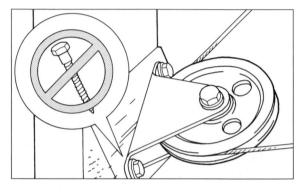

**3** Check all sheave attachments. The pressure exerted on the sheaves is substantial, and they must be through-bolted—not screwed—to adequate structural members.

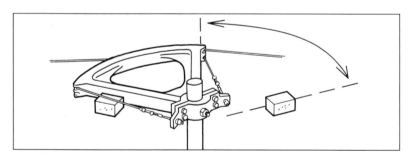

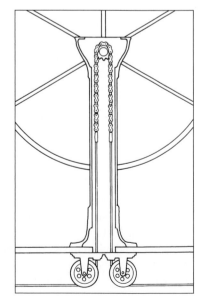

**4** Check the attachment of the quadrant to the rudderstock. No movement between the rudder and the quadrant should be possible. Solid stops should limit the quadrant movement to no more than 70 degrees.

**5** After you have made sure the cables are tight, rotate the wheel slowly from stop to stop and back. It should turn smoothly; if it is jerky, the chain and sprocket need servicing, and you will need to remove the compass to get to them.

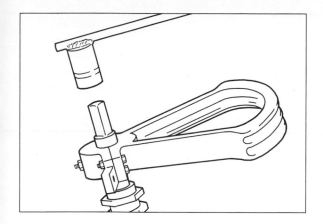

**6** Check the emergency tiller—every wheel-steered boat should have one—to make sure it fits the rudderhead and has sufficient clearance to operate properly.

## GEARED STEERING

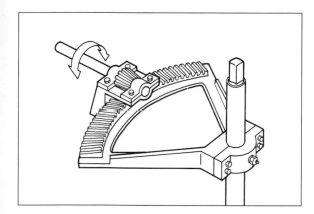

**1** With the rudder centered and held rigid, move the wheel to check for play in the worm gear or between the pinion and geared quadrant. Because wear is usually in only one area of the gear, attempts to remove the play by adjusting the mesh often fail; replacement parts are generally required.

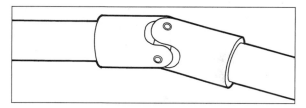

**2** Check universal joints for play. Failure to keep these joints packed in grease leads to destructive wear and corrosion.

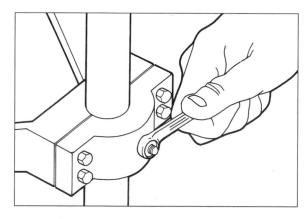

**3** Check all bolts and screws for tightness. There should be no play between the quadrant or the worm steerer and the rudderstock.

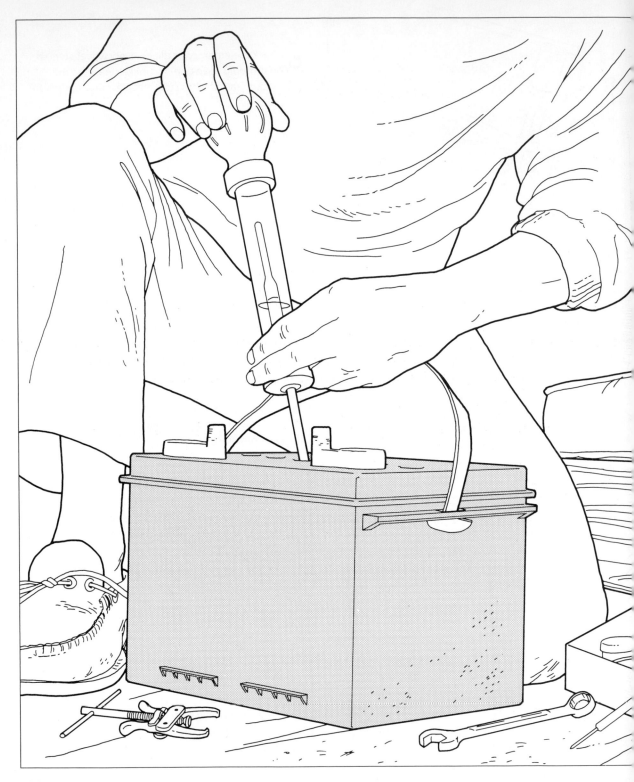

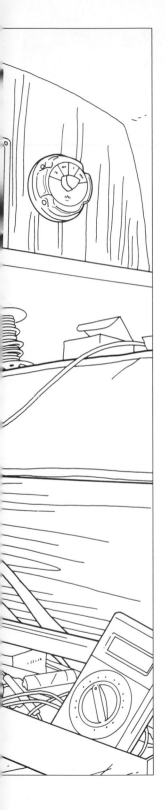

# ELECTRICAL SYSTEM

There was a time—not so long back—when newspapers reported with alarming regularity the demise of boater after boater launched into the next world by the sudden ignition of gasoline that had maliciously accumulated in the bilge. Even then the catalyst was often electrical: a spark from the battery-selector switch as the skipper routinely switched on the power.

Fortunately gasoline explosions are less common today due to more stringent engine-installation requirements, one of which is a vaporproof selector switch. But boats still catch fire and burn to the waterline, a particularly disheartening event when the shore is far away. Boat fires today are almost invariably caused by some malfunction of the electrical system, and equally invariably these disasters could have been avoided. Failure to pay close attention to a boat's electrical system is a potentially fatal error.

Even if the consequences of an electrical failure aren't as dire, it is certain to render some piece of equipment inoperable. You may find yourself ankle-deep in bilge water, in traffic lanes without running lights, or unable to start the engine. For most of us, a functioning electrical system is essential, yet there could hardly be a more unfriendly environment for electrical equipment than a boat, particularly a boat operated in salt water.

The DC electrical system of a typical sailboat is not very complicated. There may be a dozen or more circuits, but each one is essentially the same as all the others—two wires running from the battery terminals (through the main selector switch) to two terminals on the piece of electrical equipment, with a fuse or breaker in the hot (+) side of the circuit. More than one item may be connected to a given circuit, but each one is still connected across the two primary wires—like rungs between the rails of a ladder.

If the boat has a generator and AC-powered equipment aboard, extra caution is needed. AC can kill you, especially in the damp environs of a boat. Limit your survey of AC equipment to flipping switches. If the equipment doesn't work, get a qualified electrician to sort it out.

# BATTERY

Start a survey of a boat's 12-volt electrical system by examining the batteries. A separate starter battery prevents inattentive power consumption from leaving the boat without the use of the engine.

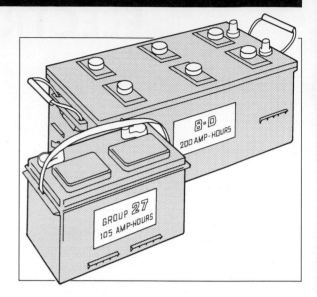

**1** Battery size and capacity have a direct relationship. Is the house battery large enough to operate the equipment aboard? For a more accurate assessment, add up the anticipated daily amp-hour consumption of the various electrical items (see sidebar); this should not exceed $\frac{1}{2}$ of the house battery's amp-hour rating. If it does, the battery is too small.

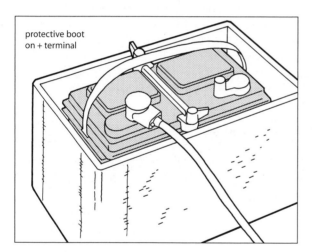

protective boot on + terminal

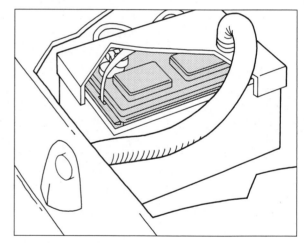

**2** Make sure the batteries are in an acidproof box and securely clamped or strapped. Sailors have been severely injured in knockdowns when a battery came adrift and fell on them.

**3** Make sure the battery locker is well ventilated. Batteries generate hydrogen gas when they are being charged, and any accumulation is an explosion risk.

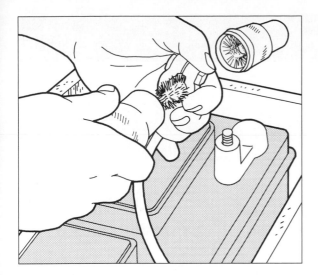

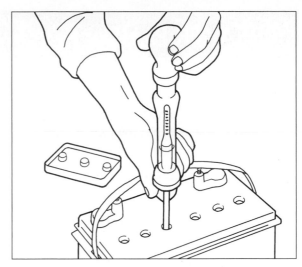

**4** Corroded terminals can stop the flow of current out of and into the battery. Terminals and cable clamps should be clean and tight. Positive terminals should be protected by a lid on the battery box or with rubber boots.

**5** To determine the condition of a wet-cell battery, check each cell with a hydrometer. A fully charged cell will have a specific gravity (SG) reading of around 1.265. If you can't charge all cells to this SG, the battery has probably lost capacity. If the highest cell reading differs by more than 0.050 from the lowest, the battery is bad.

## DAILY LOAD

A QUICK INVENTORY of the electrical equipment aboard can give you a rough idea of the necessary battery capacity. For example, a 25-watt light consumes about 2 amps (watts ÷ volts [12] = amps), or 2 amp-hours every hour. If you expect to run 4 of these lights for 4 hours each day, the amp-hour requirement is 32. For good battery life, batteries should not be discharged below 50 percent of their capacity; so 100 watts of light for 4 hours requires at least 64 amp-hours of battery capacity (limiting discharge to 30 percent will almost double battery life). Manufacturers list actual current requirements for their equipment, but here is a list of typical ratings to help you assess how well battery capacity (and charging capacity) matches the equipment aboard.

| | |
|---|---|
| Incandescent lights | 2.1 amps |
| Fluorescent lights | 0.7 |
| Fans | 1.2 |
| Masthead anchor light | 0.8 |
| Depthsounder | 0.2 |
| VHF-standby | 0.5 |
| VHF-transmit | 5.5 |
| Loran | 0.5 |
| Radar | 3.5 |
| Refrigeration | 5.5 |
| Windlass | 90.0 |
| Starter motor | 300.0 |

—courtesy of *This Old Boat*

# BREAKER PANEL

Any boat with more than one electrical circuit should be equipped with a fuse panel or breaker panel. Every circuit must be protected with a fuse or breaker. Dual batteries require a selector switch.

**1** Turn on a light and rotate the main selector switch slowly through every position. The light should come on and stay on continuously until you return to the off position. If the light flickers or goes out between positions, the switch is faulty and will ruin the alternator. The switch should be vaporproof.

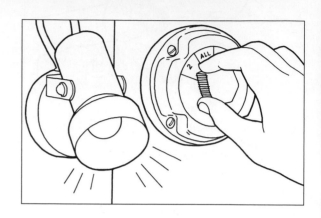

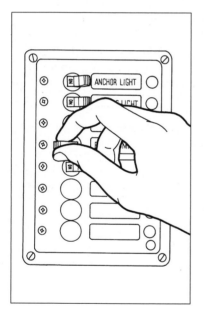

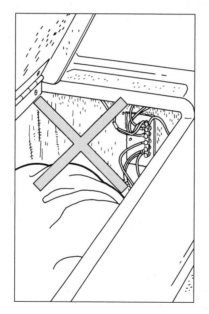

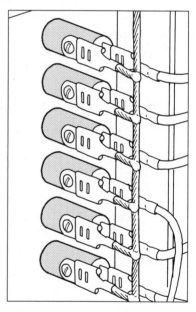

**2** Fuses are foolproof and inexpensive; breakers can make neither claim. Throw and reset each breaker on the panel to check that it operates properly.

**3** Make sure the breaker panel is not located where it can get wet. Consider the back of the panel as well; the wiring should not be exposed in a sail locker or the engine compartment.

**4** Open the breaker or fuse panel and examine the wire connections. They should be brightly soldered and neat. This often tells you a great deal about all the wiring in the boat.

# WIRE AND CONNECTORS

It isn't practical nor necessary to examine every run of wire, but making sure end connections are tight and uncorroded goes a long way toward avoiding unexpected failures. Any loose connections—not bolted to a terminal—should be sealed, preferably with heat-shrink tubing.

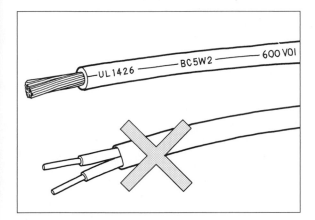

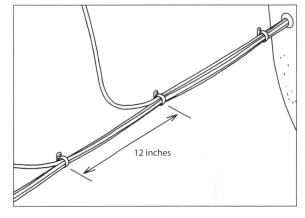

**1** Solid wire has no place on a boat. It tends to work-harden and fracture. All wiring should be stranded copper suitable for wet locations. The best is tinned Type III (Class K). This type will be labeled Marine Grade, Boat Cable, BC, BC5W2, or UL1426 on the insulation. Other acceptable wire types include MTW, AWM, THWN, and XHHW.

**2** Wire runs should be supported about every 12 inches with nonmetallic clips or ties. Look for grommets where wire passes through bulkheads and dividers.

**3** Color-coded insulation makes troubleshooting much easier. The American Boat and Yacht Council (ABYC) recommends specific colors for specific circuits, but as a practical matter, any color scheme simplifies tracing a circuit.

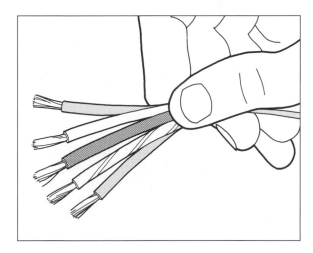

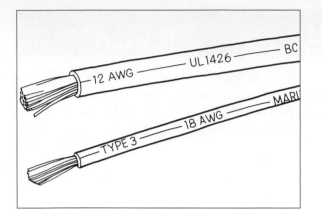

**4** Look at the wire sizes; higher loads and/or longer runs necessitate heavier gauges. Factory-installed wiring is almost always too small. In a 12-volt system, a 5-amp load 15 feet from the panel calls for #18 AWG wire if a 10-percent voltage drop is tolerable; but to deliver essentially full voltage (no more than a 3-percent drop) requires #12 AWG.

## WIRE SIZE

LIGHTS ARE TYPICALLY UNAFFECTED BY A 10-per-cent voltage drop, but most motors suffer and may not operate at all. Some electronics are also intoler-ant of low voltage. It is not necessary to immediately rewire circuits that appear to be functioning, but it is a good practice to size all new wire runs to limit the voltage drop to 3 percent. ABYC recommends nothing smaller that #16 AWG outside of a sheath (i.e., a duplex enclosure) no matter how short the run.

The wire length in the table is the distance from the panel to the device and back.

### CONDUCTOR SIZES FOR 3 PERCENT VOLTAGE DROP

| Amps at 12V | Wire run in feet | | | | | | | | | |
|---|---|---|---|---|---|---|---|---|---|---|
| | 10 | 15 | 20 | 25 | 30 | 40 | 50 | 60 | 70 | 80 |
| 5 | 18 | 16 | 14 | 12 | 12 | 10 | 10 | 10 | 8 | 8 |
| 10 | 14 | 12 | 10 | 10 | 10 | 8 | 6 | 6 | 6 | 6 |
| 15 | 12 | 10 | 10 | 8 | 8 | 6 | 6 | 6 | 4 | 4 |
| 20 | 10 | 10 | 8 | 6 | 6 | 6 | 4 | 4 | 2 | 2 |
| 25 | 10 | 8 | 6 | 6 | 6 | 4 | 4 | 2 | 2 | 2 |
| 30 | 10 | 8 | 6 | 6 | 4 | 4 | 2 | 2 | 1 | 1 |
| 40 | 8 | 6 | 6 | 4 | 4 | 2 | 2 | 1 | 0 | 0 |
| 50 | 6 | 6 | 4 | 4 | 2 | 2 | 1 | 0 | 2/0 | 2/0 |

—courtesy of *This Old Boat*

# ALTERNATOR

Alternators are generally black and white—they are either working or they aren't. A look at the ammeter when the engine is running may be the only check required, but checking the voltage at the battery is a good idea.

**1** With the alternator running, voltage measured across the charging battery should be at least 13.5 volts. If less, the alternator isn't charging.

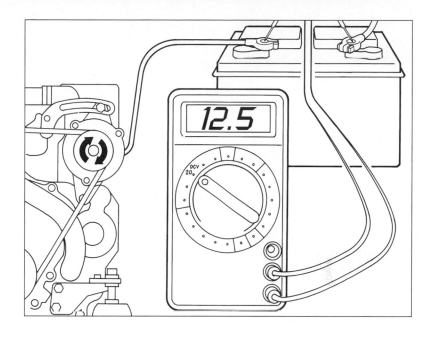

**2** If the voltage across the battery terminals is above 14.4 volts, there is a problem with the voltage regulator, and it is damaging the batteries. A rotten-egg odor is a sure sign of overcharging.

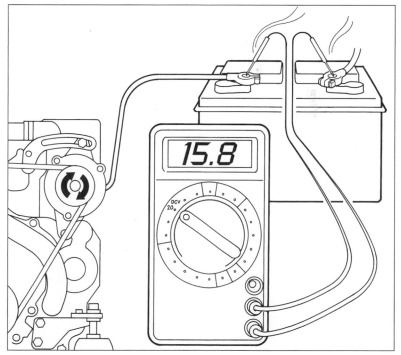

Electrical equipment, especially bilge pumps, should be checked to make sure they are working properly.

**1** Run all electrical equipment and listen for noisy bearings or erratic operation. After a few minutes of run time, touch the motor housing to check for overheating.

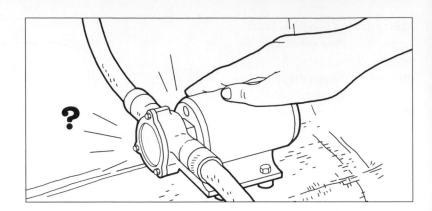

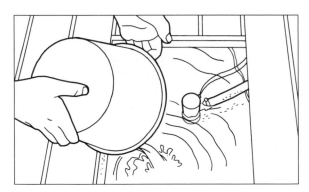

**2** Pour water into the bilge to activate the float switch on the automatic bilge pump. Never run pumps dry. Now is also a good time to make sure the discharge line is as short and straight as possible and that it's unobstructed; check valves are not desirable.

**3** Check all connections for corrosion. In wet areas like the bilge, look for the bright green corrosion that signals current leakage. Wires should never lie in water.

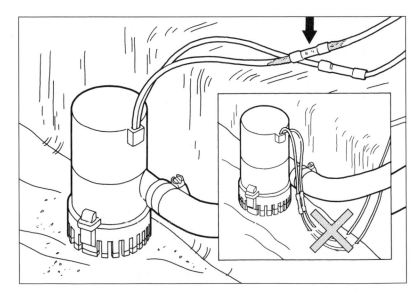

# LIGHTS

Again, the obvious test is to turn on each light to see if it works. Failure may be the fault of the bulb, the switch, the connections, the socket, or the fuse (or breaker)—generally in that order of likelihood.

**1** Unscrew incandescent bulbs and check the socket for rust. Sockets not intended for boats have steel parts that quickly disintegrate in the marine environment.

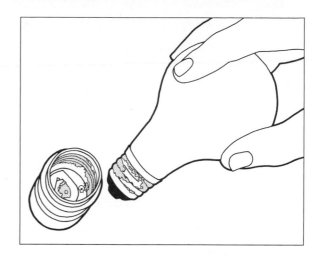

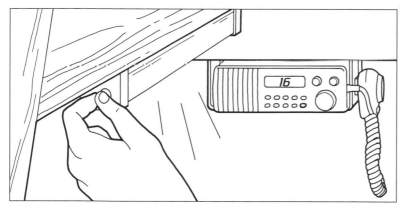

**2** With the radio and other onboard electronics operating, switch on fluorescent fixtures to check for interference. Better-quality lights have "noise" suppression circuitry but may still cause interference in certain conditions. Moving the fixture or screening the tube may be necessary.

**3** Running lights and other deck-mounted electrics need close scrutiny for corrosion of connections, sockets, and mountings.

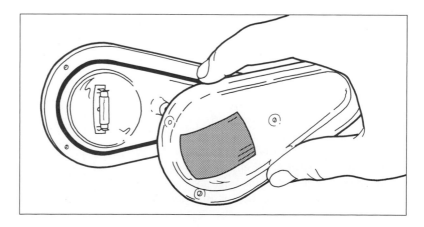

# ELECTRONICS

The lay survey of electronics is generally limited to turning on the various pieces of equipment to see if they operate properly.

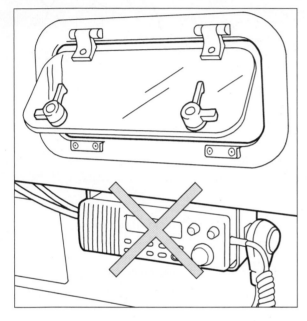

**1** Each piece of electronic gear should be located for convenient operation but out of harm's way. Even "waterproof" electronics will have fewer problems if kept dry. Direct sunlight can cause condensation to fog the inside of displays.

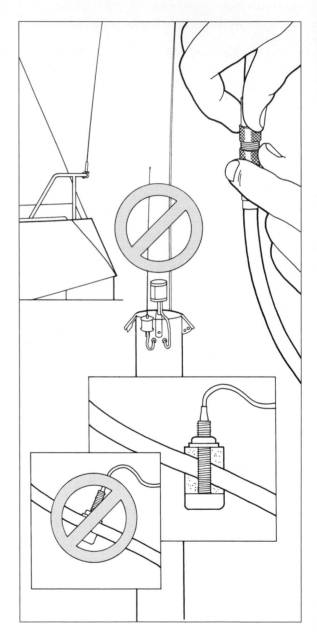

**2** Power, transducer, and antenna connections should all be tight and corrosion free. Check also the location and condition of transducers and antennas. Transducers should be properly oriented and out of turbulence. VHF antennas should be mounted as high as possible. Loran antennas should be mounted away from all other antennas.

**3** Antenna leads and power leads should not be bundled together, and neither should run near potential sources of interference—motors, fluorescent lights, and charging circuits.

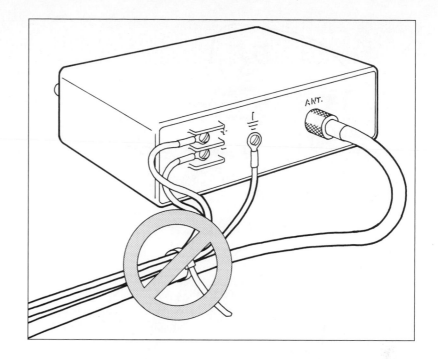

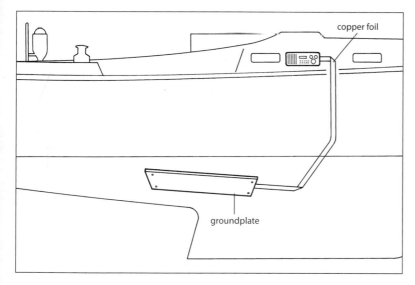

copper foil

groundplate

**4** Ham and single-sideband radios (and Loran) will not perform well without an adequate grounding system. Be sure ham and SSB radios are connected to a generous groundplate.

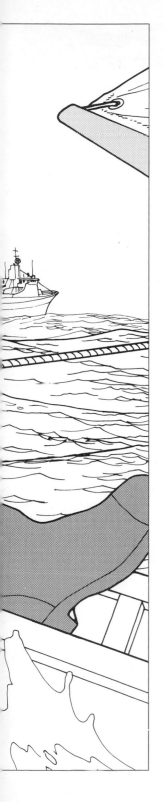

# OTHER CONSIDERATIONS

The decision to purchase a particular boat, or even the decision to invest in the boat you already own, doesn't depend entirely on the boat's condition. Suitability is a factor. If you expect to win silver, you need a boat that is fast. If you want to live aboard, a certain level of comfort is essential. If you're going to cross an ocean, reliability takes on added significance.

Some aspects of a boat assessment can take place away from the actual boat. You might read a review of this model in a consumer magazine. You might note which boats consistently lead the fleet in printed race results. You could seek out current or previous owners of sisterships. Contacting the secretary of an owner's association can be a gold mine of valuable information. Even an old press release, magazine ad, or sales brochure can sometimes be insightful: if, for example, it touts a stiffer hull in 1983, what does that say about the 1981 model you are considering?

Sometimes the name of a particular designer is expected to "say it all," but no architect gets the delicate balance of boat design exactly right every time. And to expedite production, builders often make scores of design changes without consulting or even informing the architect.

The reputation of the manufacturer can be your best clue to anticipating the quality of a boat, but boat companies change hands. Commitment to quality can easily change with ownership—or just due to economic reality.

The price of a boat is rarely much affected by the inventory of equipment aboard, but quality equipment in good condition does add to the value of the boat. If you are comparing two or more similar boats, a list of the included equipment should be part of your assessment. For your own boat, a comprehensive equipment survey will save you trouble and money in the event of an insurance claim.

# DESIGN

Despite phenomenal advances in the textile industry, it remains true that you can't make a silk purse out of a sow's ear. And no matter how well built or meticulously maintained, a tub is still a tub.

**1** Honestly assess how you will use a boat. A fat double-ender is poorly suited for summer weekends on Long Island Sound. Don't consider an 8-foot draft if you're planning an Intracoastal trip to the Bahamas. Adding weather cloths to a lightly built club racer doesn't make it a bluewater cruiser. And a retired ocean-racing greyhound is a poor cruiser choice for a retired husband and wife.

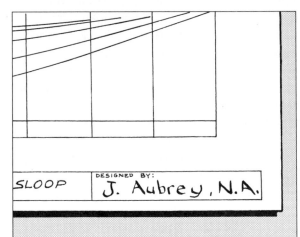

**2** Who is the designer? Does his reputation mesh with your needs; i.e., is the designer known for drawing flyers, bay sailers, or passagemakers? Is this one of his better designs? A telephone call to a still-working designer can answer questions you may not even know to ask.

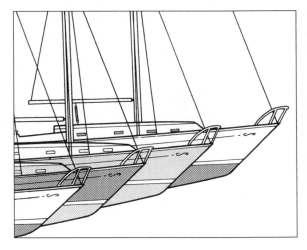

**3** How many of these boats were built? A long production run suggests an especially successful design, a valuable recommendation if the boat suits your needs.

# REPUTATION

Boats tend to earn a reputation. They are "sweet" or "bulletproof" or "junk." Builders likewise become known for the kinds of boats they turn out.

**1** Talk to other sailors about the boats you are considering. Don't depend on a single "expert"; individual opinions are shaded by personal preferences. Talk to various sailors, ask "Why?" often, and look for consensus.

**2** Sailboat manufacturers come and go. That a boat manufacturer is no longer in business reflects only on their business skills, not the quality of their boats. Some built terrible boats that disappeared with the company. Just as many built excellent boats, finding themselves unable to compete against cheaper offerings. The fate of the manufacturer is of little practical consequence to the owner of an older sailboat.

# PERFORMANCE

Speed may not seem important, but sitting still while other boats glide by will soon tarnish a sailboat's other merits. Even a barge will sail when the wind pipes up, so to find out how well a boat sails, take her out in light air. For a bluewater boat, heavy-air performance is equally important, suggesting a second sea trial.

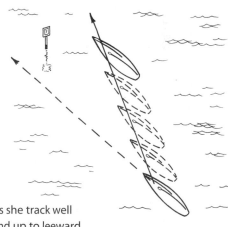

**1** Does the boat balance well, or does she want to round up if you ease your pull on the tiller?

**2** Does she track well or end up to leeward of the compass course?

**3** Is she easy to sail, or does cranking in the genoa sheet test your strength?

**4** How close to the wind will she keep moving well? This is half the angle between tacks.

45°

lower tacking angles are better

45°

WIND

**5** An ocean vessel should carry sail and remain dry in moderate conditions.

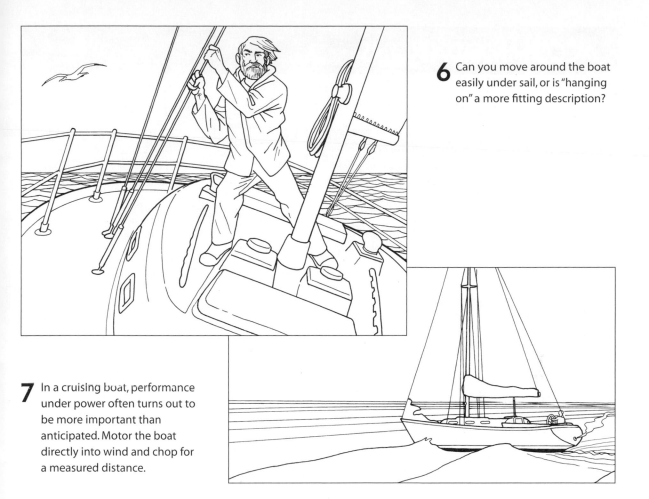

**6** Can you move around the boat easily under sail, or is "hanging on" a more fitting description?

**7** In a cruising boat, performance under power often turns out to be more important than anticipated. Motor the boat directly into wind and chop for a measured distance.

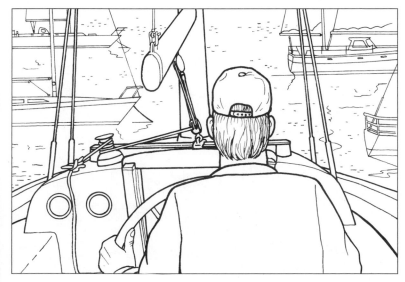

**8** How does she handle under power in close quarters?

For the inexperienced sailor, sea trials have limited value as a boat evaluation tool. If you are a neophyte, give more weight to the boat's reputation. In other words, buy a boat that you know is capable and its performance will improve with your skills.

# ACCOMMODATIONS

If you plan to "live" on the boat—overnight or longer—then the accommodation plan also needs to perform. We have already assessed the construction and safety of various cabin features ("Interior"); here we are talking about how well the design fits your needs.

**1** Will every crewmember have a comfortable bunk and adjacent storage for clothes and other belongings?

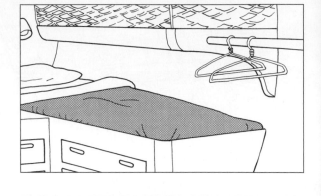

**2** Will the table seat everyone comfortably at mealtimes?

**3** Does the galley make turning out a multicourse meal a joy or a chore?

**4** Is the cabin a cozy, dry, and well-ventilated haven for the entire crew in inclement weather? Can everyone move around, or is the only passage often blocked by the table or the cook?

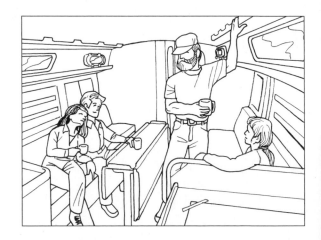

# EQUIPMENT

Because you may be tempted to depend on it, poor equipment is worse than no equipment. Check the gear aboard for quality, condition, and suitability.

**1** Good ground tackle is essential for a cruising sailboat. Anchors should be ample in size and suitable in type for the expected bottom conditions. Check chains for corrosion, lines for abrasion, shackles for bent pins and absent safety wire.

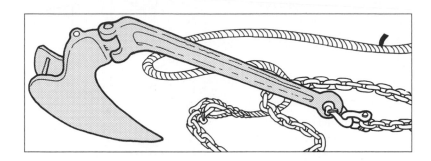

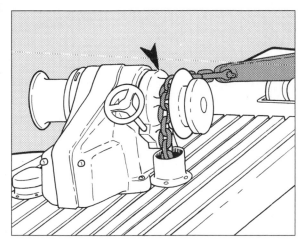

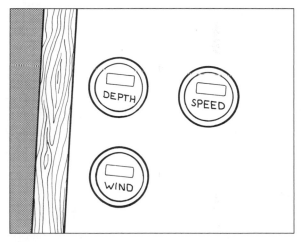

**2** When the ground tackle is heavy, a functioning windlass is essential. Make sure the wildcat or gypsy fits the chain aboard.

**3** Most boats of any size are equipped with some electronic gear. A VHF radio and a depthsounder are almost always useful. The value of other electronics depends entirely on whether you will use them.

**4** Coast Guard safety gear is essential. Make sure the boat is equipped with fire extinguishers, life jackets, and the necessary flares and horns.

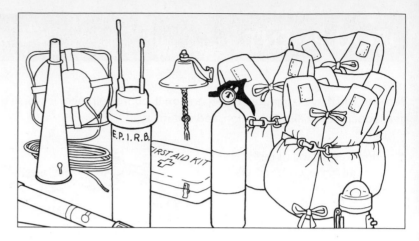

**5** Lockers should contain adequate fenders and docklines and a sturdy boathook.

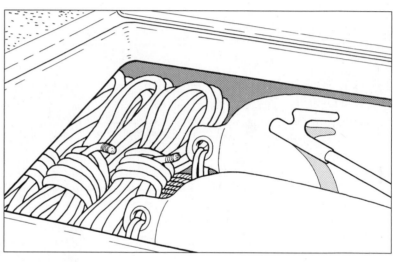

**6** List other gear like liferafts, dinghies, awnings, cushions, flags, windscoops, swim ladder, and bosun's chair. Anything aboard in good condition that you would otherwise buy gives the boat added value for you.

gear aboard

Avon Redcrest—good condition
6 hp Johnson—tired
6-man Switlik raft in cannister
2 harnesses
canvas bosun's chair—
    good condition

# VALUE

The value of a boat to you is whatever you're willing to pay for it; but for the purchase to be a sound investment, you don't want to pay too much. The trick is to figure out how much the seller thinks the boat is worth—a number that tends to decrease the longer the boat is on the market.

**1** BUC Research semiannually publishes their *Used Boat Guide*, which lists market values for most production boats built in the last 30 years. However, unless recent sales of a specific boat have been reported, the guide's price may be out-of-date. BUC also gets its information from brokers and dealers, who have been known to misreport sale prices to keep the BUC value up.

**2** NADA has long published used car prices, but only recently ventured into the used boat arena with their *Used Boat Price Guide*. Far fewer boat sales preclude the level of accuracy of the car guide, particularly for sailboats, but this guide can provide another clue to a boat's value.

**3** Look in newspapers and magazines for advertisements for similar boats. Look at back issues as well as current ones; values of older boats change slowly. Keep in mind that the listed price is what the seller is asking. Selling price is likely to be 10 to 20 percent less, sometimes lower.

**4** As with real estate, yacht brokers subscribe to a listing service. A cooperative broker can provide you with the asking price of every boat of a particular type offered for sale by any participating broker—which is most brokers in North America and the Caribbean, and beyond.

**5** *Practical Sailor* has occasionally published a comparative chart of used boat prices. Again, these are asking prices, but the value of the chart is that it suggests relative values, allowing you to get more information from ads. For example, if the chart shows boat B is worth about 25 percent less than boat A, and there are three boat As in the newspaper for 20 grand, a $15,000 asking price is about right for a boat B.

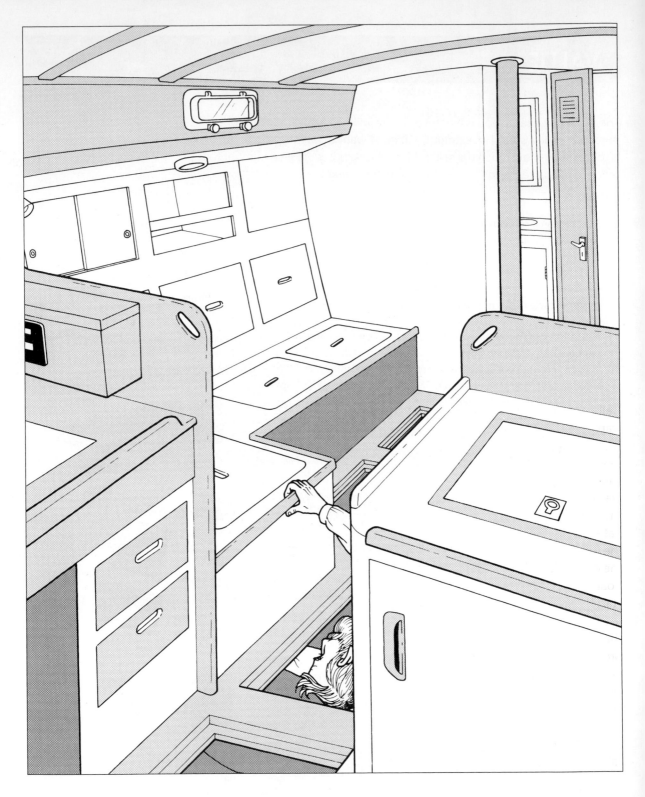

# BOAT-BUYER'S 30-MINUTE SURVEY

The process of buying a used boat can be overwhelming. You look at one boat, then another, then another. To bring some order to this effort, most shoppers settle on one boat early on that becomes the standard. Subsequent boats are compared and eliminated if they don't displace the standard. This scheme works pretty well, but the problem is the basis for selecting the standard.

Sailboat buyers tend to make their selection based mostly on how a boat looks and how sumptuous the interior is. If the boat selected this way surveys well, everything is fine. But suppose the surveyor reports that the cored hull is delaminated so extensively that repair costs will exceed the value of the boat. At the very least you're out the cost of the survey, and if you ranked the other boats only against the standard, you may have to start all over.

Of course if you did your own assessment of the selected boat prior to commissioning a professional, you would have found the delamination and saved the cost of a survey. That puts money back in your pocket, but still leaves you back at square one as far as buying a boat. You either have to make a second pick from memory—hardly a good plan—or you have to take a second look at all the candidates.

What if you had discovered the hull delamination the first time you looked at the chosen boat? You wouldn't now be facing the prospect of setting up appointments to take a second look at a bunch of boats you're not going to buy. Look at boats squint-eyed rather than wide-eyed and you will minimize the number of surprises when you come back to your top choice or two for a closer examination.

It is impractical to fully assess every boat you look at, but about 30 minutes of focused scrutiny will catch all the obvious problems and give you a good idea of the overall quality and condition of the boat. The trick is to know exactly what you're looking for and not allow yourself to be distracted by joinerwork and varnish. Remember that you're not trying to learn the condition of everything; if the boat passes muster, you'll be back.

Boats are almost always consistent, so if your quick survey turns up quality or maintenance problems, these are likely to be representative. However, bear in mind that if a boat has passed through several hands, repairs and modifications may reflect the differing levels of skill and/or care of the various owners.

To do a quick survey, you'll need a good flashlight and either a thin-blade screwdriver or a plastic-handled awl. Take a pen and pad to record your findings.

# HULL

A boat has to have eye appeal or you won't be happy with it, but don't fall in love. A pretty shape should just qualify a boat for consideration. Conversely, if you hate the lines, save everyone's time and don't even go aboard.

**1** **Topsides.** Keeping the side of your face just clear of the topsides, walk quickly around the hull. You are looking for irregularities in the surface—bumps, flat spots, hardspots, or damage. Also watch the flow of the hull-to-deck joint for signs of separation.

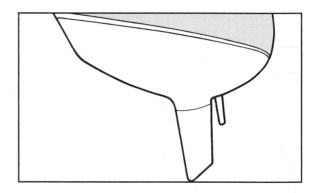

**2** **Bottom.** Make a second, slower pass around the boat, this time examining the bottom. Look particularly for signs of blisters—bumps—or blister repairs—flat spots—but note any flaw that catches your eye.

**3** **Keel.** If there is a keel joint, check it for tightness. Examine the leading edge and bottom of the keel for signs of hard grounding.

**4** **Hull delamination.** With the handle of your screwdriver, tap the hull around all through-hull fittings, including transducers and rudder fittings, and in the area of any flaws you noted in your two circuits of the hull. These are the likely places for delamination to start.

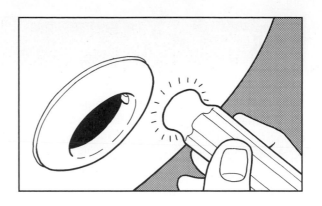

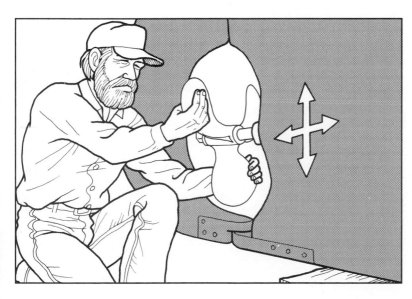

**5** **Rudder.** Push on the trailing edge of the rudder to see if it operates smoothly; look for movement between the shell and the stock. Shake the leading edge to check the pintles and rudder tube for play.

**6** **Prop.** Shake the prop to check the Cutless bearing. Note the condition of the prop.

# DECK

If you discover problems in your examination of the hull that eliminate this boat from consideration, you can stop there. Otherwise, it is time to go aboard. Out of courtesy and to broaden your exposure to boats, you may want to go aboard anyway.

**1** **Deck delamination.** Start at the bow and sound the deck and cabintop about every foot or two with the handle of your screwdriver. Most old fiberglass sailboats have some delamination in the deck; you are looking for a big problem.

**2** **Bedding.** As you sound your way around the deck, look for beads of silicone or other caulk along toerails and around window frames. This is a sure sign of leakage in these areas.

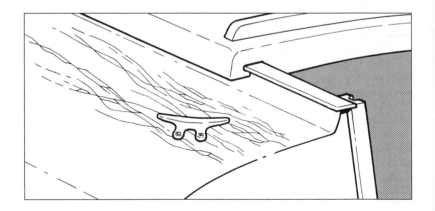

**3** **Gelcoat cracks.** Also keep an eye out for stress cracks in the gelcoat as you sound. Large areas of stress cracking are likely to respond to your tapping with the dull thud of delamination.

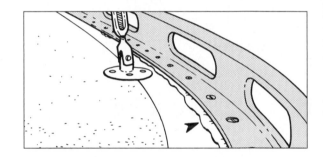

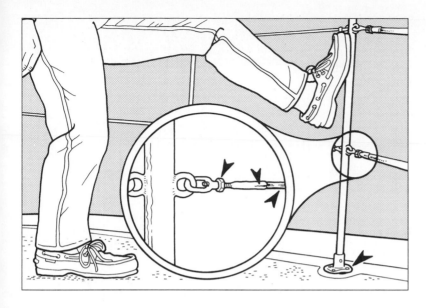

**4** **Stanchions and lifelines.** Check stanchions to see if they are erect and sturdy. Check the end fittings on lifelines for corrosion and cracking. Also note any rust stains breaking through the plastic coating.

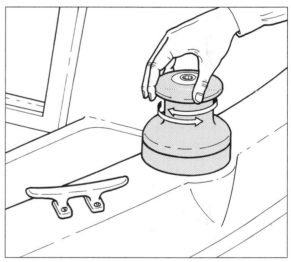

**6** **Winches.** Rotate each winch once around, listening for the regular musical click of pawls that will suggest that the winch is clean and appropriately lubricated.

**5** **Helm.** Move the tiller or turn the wheel to check for binding or play.

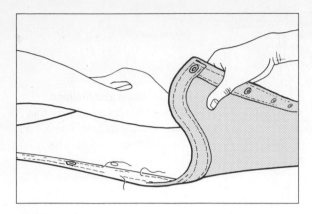

**7** **Canvas.** Give all the canvas on deck a quick once-over, observing vibrancy and feeling the cloth for age clues. Check the stitching and look for chafe and tears.

**8** **Working sails.** Uncover any sail stowed on a boom. It isn't necessary to spread the sail; you can guess its condition by examining the leech near a batten pocket. Pull out the first 3 or 4 feet of a roller-furled sail for the same reason. Also note if the sail rolls out and back in easily.

# RIG

Before you go below, take a quick look at the rig. You are mainly looking for damage or corrosion, but it takes no additional time to note the mast section and wire diameter in order to get a feel for how strongly the boat is rigged.

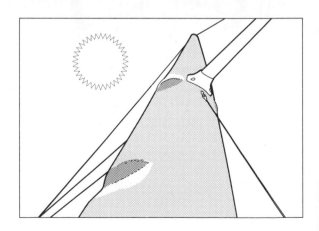

**1** **Mast.** Sight up the mast to see if it is straight. Look for dimples or ridges. Note the condition of the protective finish.

**2** **Step.** Inspect the base of a deck-stepped mast for signs of corrosion. Note also the condition of the step and the contour of the deck; dishing around the step suggests inadequate mast support.

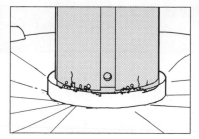

**3** **Spreaders.** From the stern, see if the tip elevation of port and starboard spreaders match. Do the spreaders bisect the angle the shroud makes as it passes over the tip? Move the upper shrouds vigorously fore and aft, watching the spreader bases to see if they are solidly attached to the mast.

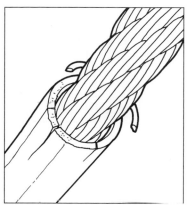

**4** **Rigging.** If lower end fittings are swaged, make a quick inspection of each one to see if it is cracked or bent. Also check the wire near the swage for broken strands. When the end fittings are mechanical, check the wire only.

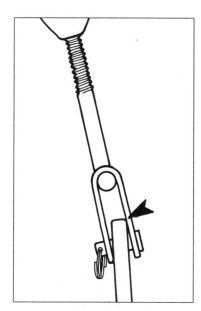

**5** **Chainplates.** As you check end fittings, note also the size and condition of the chainplates. Are they properly aligned with the attached shroud or stay?

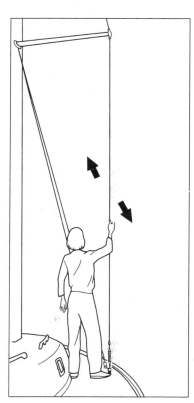

# BELOW

It is time to go below. Take a minute or two to take in the layout and note any special features, but then get right back to your examination. Start at the forepeak and work aft, peering into every compartment and lighting its dark recesses with your flashlight to check (for) the following:

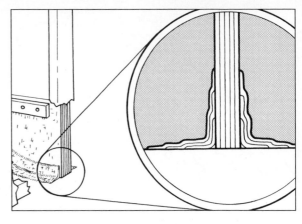

**1 Leaks.** Look for salt crystals, dust rivulets, and water stains. Tracks high on the hull are usually from deck-joint problems; other leaks are less serious if they haven't already caused damage.

**2 Tabbing.** Find access to some bulkhead tabbing and check it. Bulkheads should be tabbed on both sides with several layers. Plastic laminate should have been removed in the tabbing area. The tabbing should extend onto the bulkhead at least 3 inches—more as boats get larger. Check with your screwdriver to see that it is attached.

**3 Chainplates.** Chainplates should be accessible and through-bolted to strong structural members. Inaccessible chainplates prevent assurance that they are in good condition.

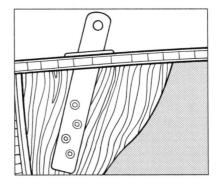

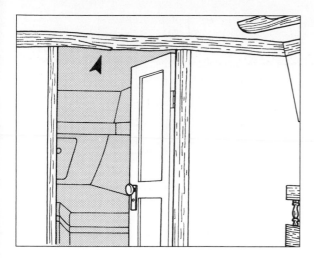

**4** **Mast support.** Check the bulkhead or beam that supports a deck-stepped mast; it should be solid and undistorted. If the mast is keel-stepped, check the supporting floors for cracks or rot. Also examine the step and mast base for corrosion.

**5** **Door alignment.** Look at cabin and cabinet doors. Some misalignment is common, but if the door jams or has been trimmed, the hull is flexing and wrenching the bulkheads.

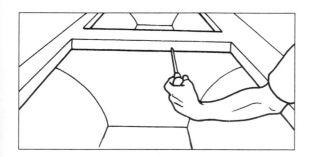

**6** **Rot.** Tap around the edges of the cabin sole and at the bottom of bulkheads. If you get a dull report, try the pointed end of your awl or screwdriver on the wood. Check wooden engine bearers.

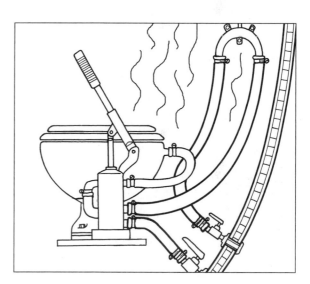

**7** **Head.** Is the head installation legal? Is the toilet dry and clean or leaky and disgusting?

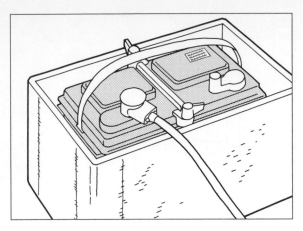

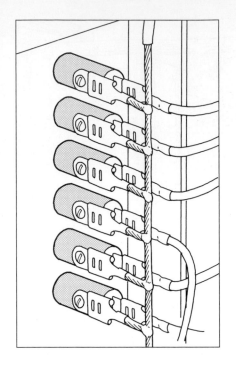

**8** **Batteries.** If the batteries are in the boat, are they clean and are the terminals corrosion free? How old are they?—they generally have a date on them. Common deep-cycle batteries rarely last much longer than 5 years; heavy-duty marine batteries can last 10 years or more.

**9** **Electrics.** If the face of the switch panel is hinged, open it and look inside. Otherwise check the electrical wiring in two or three locations for size, type, and support, and for the condition of the connections. Switch on each electrical item as you work your way through the cabin.

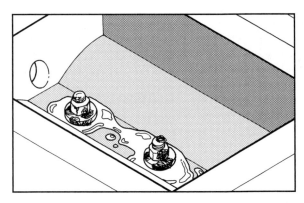

**10** **Through-hull fittings.** Do you observe any through-hulls with gate valves or no valve at all? Do seacocks appear clean and operational or green and frozen? The flange of a properly installed seacock will be through-bolted on a flat surface.

**11** **Keel bolts.** Pull up the floorboards and look at the keel bolts for corrosion or signs of leakage. Note if the material under the washers or backing plates is solid or cracked.

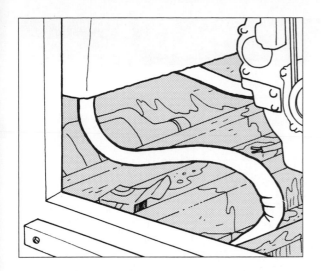

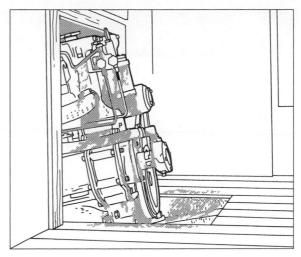

**12** **Bilge.** Is the bilge clean and dry or full of oil and debris? Is the boat equipped with a manual bilge pump in addition to the electric one, and do both have short, straight discharge runs?

**13** **Engine.** Is the engine a rusting lump or painted and clean? Is the compartment black with oil or belt dust? Rub across the underside of engine surfaces and fuel pumps to check for fresh leaks.

**14** **Other sails.** Pull a corner of each sail out of its bag and see if the cloth has lost its body or if the edges show chafe or fraying.

# IMPRESSION

Before you leave the boat, make a note of any significant findings. Now is also a good time to categorize this boat.

**1 Classic or condo.** First-time boat buyers tend to look at sailboats in terms of how much space they have. Think a minute about the boats that attracted you to sailing. Is this boat destined to be a classic, or is it a floating condo?

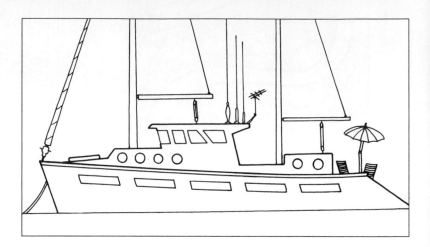

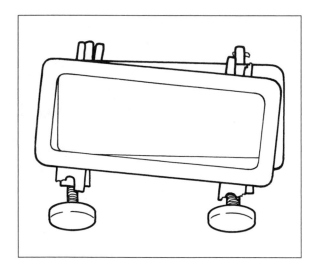

**2 Quality or budget.** Now that you've pulled, poked, and prodded, determine for yourself if the manufacturer cut corners to hold the cost down. Is the hardware plastic, the interior finish of the glass rough? Are the portlights going to break the first time someone dogs them down tight?

**3 Light or heavy.** For protected waters you want a boat light enough to sail well but not so light that you worry about the hull cracking like an egg. For offshore sailing you want a boat heavy enough to take the punishment of a storm, but not so heavy that you need a storm to make her sail. How would you characterize the construction of this boat?

**4** **Use or neglect.** It is important to determine whether a boat is showing her age because she has been used or because she's been neglected. Use suggests that, at the very least, essential maintenance has been done; surprises are less likely. Neglect gives various destructive forces an opportunity to gain a foothold; long-term neglect is almost always costly.

# HIRING A PROFESSIONAL

If you are 99 percent sure that the boat you are buying is sound, why do you need to spend the money on a professional survey?

Well, first there is that 1 percent. But even if you like the odds, chances are a survey is going to be required. If you plan to insure an aging sailboat, expect the insurance company to require a current survey. If you need financing for your purchase, the bank is also likely to demand proof of the value of your floating collateral. And even if they don't demand a survey, they will require insurance. You can see where that leads. So if you have to pay for a survey anyway, it makes incontrovertible sense to have it done before the problems it turns up are yours.

Perhaps a more compelling argument for having a professional survey is that it is likely to save instead of cost you money. When the value of a boat is in the thousands of dollars, most sellers expect any purchase agreement to be contingent upon a satisfactory survey. The seller will have to correct significant flaws or at the very least renegotiate the selling price, and the dollars involved often far exceed the survey cost.

Can't the seller refuse and let the deal collapse? Sure, but even if you go away as a buyer, the seller knows the problems with the boat won't. Unless the survey is awful—and it shouldn't be if you've already checked out the boat carefully—there is usually a genuine desire on the part of both parties to hold the deal together. Sometimes the owner knows the boat has undisclosed problems, but probably more often the survey findings are news. It can take a couple of days for the owner to assimilate this new knowledge and come to grips with the fact that his or her boat is worth less than originally thought. Patience and a willingness to cut the seller a little slack can lead to a transaction that satisfies both parties.

A third reason for a survey is that the professional surveyor has no vested interest. When you have really fallen for a particular boat, the rose-colored glasses can be thick enough to blind you to her faults. Seeing them listed in black and white can be just the slap you need.

## FINDING A COMPETENT SURVEYOR

Marine surveying is an unregulated service. A flyer on the marina bulletin board or a listing in the Yellow Pages is all that is needed to get into the business. But because someone calls themselves a surveyor doesn't mean they really are one. A significant percentage of so-called professional surveys aren't worth the paper they are printed on, much less the hundreds of dollars the "surveyor" charged. In a medical system that didn't require training, internship, or licensing for doctors, would you select a pediatrician at random from telephone listings, or would you check with other parents? Finding a good surveyor requires a bit of effort, but it will be time well invested.

Sometimes finding a surveyor is easy; you ask around at the marina and one name keeps coming up.

But more often, asking other boatowners just elicits a shrug. A boatowner that hasn't changed boats in a few years has little reason to be current on surveyors.

Ask the manager of the boatyard you use. Boatyard operators see surveyors at work all the time. They hear sellers complain about nit-picking, buyers complain about dependability or overcharging. They are asked to do work that isn't needed and later see problems that a survey should have picked up. But boatyard managers sometimes see surveying as an appropriate sideline business, given their expertise. Because of the potential conflict of interest—more findings mean more work for the yard—the two U.S. surveying associations (see below) strictly prohibit surveyors from being engaged in the boatyard business (or as brokers or marine vendors). However, only about 20 percent of surveyors belong to a professional association, so such by-laws have no significance for the other 80 percent.

Brokers always have a list of surveyors they can recommend. Keep in mind, though, that it is in the broker's best interest for the survey to be clean, so a local surveyor known for her thoroughness may be purposely omitted from your broker's list. Never accept a single recommendation from a broker, and carefully check out all surveyors recommended by the broker before making a selection.

There are two professional associations for surveyors in the U.S.—the National Association of Marine Surveyors and the Society of Accredited Marine Surveyors. Both can provide listings of member surveyors in your area. Membership is no assurance that a surveyor is competent, but these associations do have minimum experience requirements. They also sponsor periodic seminars and recommend uniform survey practices. A surveyor who is a member of NAMS or SAMS usually notes this in ads and on business cards. Contact NAMS at 1-800-822-NAMS; reach SAMS at 1-800-344-9077. SAMS also has a home page on the Internet that lists all its members; the address is *http://www.yachtsales.com/listings/SAMS/p&ht.html*.

Another source of surveyor recommendations is your insurance agent. No matter how you come to choose a surveyor, you should make sure that the survey will be acceptable to both your lender and your insurer before you have it done. Insurers especially can have defined survey requirements, and if the survey you provide fails to meet their requirements, they may refuse to accept it. Select your surveyor from a list provided by your agent and you avoid this situation.

Being on the agent's list may be the best recommendation anyway. Unlike the broker, the boatyard operator, or even other sailors, the insurance company shares your keen interest in finding out everything that is wrong with this boat, especially anything that might cost money or result in personal injury. Start your search with a call to your insurance agent, then confirm your choice by checking accreditations and recommendations.

## COST

Costs vary geographically, and like the price of almost every other service, they tend to rise over time. Currently you should anticipate being charged between $10 and $12 per foot for a sailboat under 40 feet, and up to about $15 per foot for boats larger than that. (As boats get longer they also get wider and more complicated.)

Many surveyors also charge travel time, including billing you for mileage. If you want the surveyor to participate in a sea trial, there is likely to be an hourly charge for that. If the boat is in the water, add haulout costs of $3 to $4 per foot. Few surveyors are qualified to determine the condition of the engine, so expect to spend another $300 to $400 if you want the engine thoroughly inspected.

Adding everything up, $20 to $25 per foot for both boat and machinery will give you a fair estimate of actual out-of-pocket cost. An $800 survey adds 10 percent to the cost of an $8,000 35-footer but only 1 percent if the boat's price is $80,000. And you are likely to pay for the survey in the first case since the price is already at the bottom of the range at $8,000; but almost any flaw discovered in the second case will lower the selling price by more than $800. That means there is no real cost to the buyer in the latter case; the survey actually saves the buyer money.

The actual monetary cost or benefit of a survey varies; the constant is that a survey inserts a known cost into the equation and takes out surprise costs. If you aren't required by an insurer or lender to survey the boat, then you have to evaluate the cost against the potential benefit. If the survey cost doesn't exceed 2 percent of the contract price, having the boat surveyed will almost always save you money.

## WHAT TO EXPECT

Survey reports can be long or short. They can be informative or simply descriptive. They can be narrative or multiple choice. They can describe all of a boat's faults or only those due to wear and tear.

Surveyors tend to follow a pattern in all their surveys, so ask a prospective surveyor for a sample survey to make sure you will be getting the information you want. Be cautious of long surveys that list every item aboard and comment on the condition of everything. Better surveyors confine their comments to things that need pointing out.

Since you have already looked the boat over carefully, it is a good idea to tell the surveyor about any specific concerns. If you are worried about blisters or bulkhead attachments or the strength of the rudder tube, ask the surveyor to comment on those items.

Ask your surveyor if he or she has ever surveyed a sistership to the boat you are considering. A surveyor with extensive prior experience with this model may know what trouble to be especially on the lookout for.

You should also tell the surveyor how you plan to use the boat. Knowing, for example, that you expect to take this particular boat offshore, your surveyor might comment on rigging-wire size and mast section where he might otherwise have ignored these deficiencies (for your intended use) simply because they are standard for this particular boat.

Most surveyors would probably prefer to be left alone to concentrate on the job at hand, but attending the survey will be instructive for you and allow you to get detailed explanations of significant findings. If you want to be there while the boat is surveyed, tell your prospective surveyor up front. If it is clear you aren't welcome, you may be happier with a different surveyor.

Expect your surveyor to spend several hours aboard, to wriggle into every space and compartment, and to give you a written report within a couple of days of the survey. The report should reflect his or her findings in adequate detail and offer recommendations to correct any deficiencies. If you request it, a valuation will also be a part of the report.

If repairs will be made prior to closing the sale, plan on bringing the surveyor back to inspect the work.

# INDEX

**The McGraw·Hill Companies**

21 LCR 23

© 1997, 2005 by International Marine

*The Library of Congress has cataloged the cloth edition as follows:*

Casey, Don.
    Inspecting the aging sailboat / Don Casey.
        p.     cm.—(The International Marine sailboat library)
     ISBN 0-07-013394-8
     1. Sailboats—Maintenance and repair. I. Title.
     II. Series.
    VM531.C327 1996
    623.8'223'0288—dc20                 96-26741
                                     CIP

Paperback ISBN 0-07-144545-5

Questions regarding the content of this book should be addressed to
    International Marine
    P.O. Box 220
    Camden, ME 04843
    www.internationalmarine.com

Questions regarding the ordering of this book should be addressed to
    The McGraw-Hill Companies
    Customer Service Department
    P.O. Box 547
    Blacklick, OH 43004
    Retail customers: 1-800-262-4729
    Bookstores: 1-800-722-4726

Illustrations in chapters 1, 2, 4, and 7 by Rob Groves.
Illustrations in chapters 3, 5, and 6 by Jim Sollers.

DON CASEY credits the around-the-world-voyage of Robin Lee Graham, featured in *National Geographic* in the late sixties, with opening his eyes to the world beyond the shoreline. After graduating from the University of Texas he moved to south Florida, where he began to spend virtually all his leisure time messing about in boats.

In 1983 he abandoned a career in banking to devote more time to cruising and writing. His work combining these two passions soon began to appear in many popular sailing and boating magazines. In 1986 he co-authored *Sensible Cruising: The Thoreau Approach*, an immediate best-seller and the book responsible for pushing many would-be cruisers over the horizon. He is also author of *This Old Boat*, a universally praised guide that has led thousands of boatowners through the process of turning a rundown production boat into a first-class yacht, and of *Sailboat Refinishing*, *Sailboat Hull & Deck Repair*, and *Canvaswork & Sail Repair*, part of the International Marine Sailboat Library. He continues to evaluate old and new products and methods, often trying them on his own 27-year-old, much-modified, Allied Seawind.

When not writing or off cruising, he can be found sailing on Florida's Biscayne Bay.

## THE INTERNATIONAL MARINE SAILBOAT LIBRARY

*Inspecting the Aging Sailboat* has company:

**Boatowner's Handbook**
*by John Vigor*

**Canvaswork & Sail Repair**
*by Don Casey*

**100 Fast & Easy Boat Improvements**
*by Don Casey*

**Sailboat Hull & Deck Repair**
*by Don Casey*

**Sailboat Refinishing**
*by Don Casey*

**Troubleshooting Marine Diesels**
*by Peter Compton*